Only Jesus

*Jesus Christ The One
and Only Savior*

Dr. Ebbie Smith continues to produce work that is worthy of study and helpful to the body of Christ. His most recent book gives a thorough, scholarly, yet readable explanation of how many people in our culture understand salvation. In his thorough treatment of various ways of understanding salvation, he sets forth a clear and convincing understanding for an exclusivistic view of salvation with passion. He speaks about how believers with broken hearts must accept the lostness of humankind apart from Christ and His Gospel. I encourage you to read this book, listen to it and learn from it. In the 21st century, there is increased division, even in the body of Christ, about the truths of God's Word. This book will help set a clear understanding.

Dr. Frank Page

President and Chief Executive Officer
SBC Executive Committee
901 Commerce Street, Nashville, TN 37203

With theological precision and motivating passion Dr. Ebbie Smith addresses an issue that has been reconfigured and become controverted during the past quarter century: Is Jesus the only Savior? He carefully delineates eschatological universalism, pluralism, inclusivism, and particularism and identifies varieties of particularism. The result is a helpful guide through a complex issue.

Dr. James Leo Garrett, Jr.

Distinguished Professor of Theology, Emeritus
Southwestern Baptist Theological Seminary

Dr. Ebbie Smith's *Only Jesus* is a tractate for the times, a clarion call to evangelism in the midst of a bewildering world of 'isms'. He tackles the question of how the traditional witness of the Christian gospel addresses the emerging influence of religious pluralism and especially the increasing militancy of world religions. By definition, summary, and comparison, the distinctive positions are sketched out for all sides of the house that are, in one way or another, attempts to deal with the question of the fate of the unevangelized. Smith makes the scriptural case for traditional theism with its exclusive emphasis on the gospel in the face of less acceptable options in world religion circles.

Chief among the features of the book is a mandate: putting aside the arguments, the church on mission must courageously engage the task of witness. Mission strategy must be built on revelation not speculation—the Bible is clear about the mystery of sin and the dilemma of mankind; the strategy must be built on proclamation not desperation— the Bible's confident, triumphal strains endorse the power and effectiveness of the gospel as the saving power of God. This book is readable, sane, and demanding—a gripping word for practitioners of the faith!

Dr. Bruce Corley

President
Professor of New Testament and Greek
B. H. Carroll Theological Institute
301 S. Center St., Suite 100
Arlington, TX 76010

Dr. Ebbie Smith just does not know when to quit! Officially retired from a long and productive career as Professor of Missions and Ethics at SWBTS, he continues to study and write on pertinent theological subjects. Here is a masterful book on Christian apologetics, wonderfully documented. As his longtime colleague, I wish to commend him on addressing and critiquing these attempts to play down the finality of Jesus Christ. The finality of Jesus Christ is without question, the essence of the Christian world mission.

Dr. Justice C. Anderson

Professor of Missions, Emeritus
SWBTS, Fort Worth, Texas. 20ll

Ebbie Smith has demonstrated his commitment to evangelism and missions through his service as missionary and teacher. In Only Jesus: Jesus Christ the One and Only Savior, Smith contributes to evangelism and missions by his clear stand on the basic doctrine of Salvation in Christ alone. The book approaches an important subject that needs a clarifying voice in our day. Clearly, as Smith writes, we cannot count on any teaching not taught in the biblical revelation nor can we hold out any promise not in the revelation from God.

Dr. Daniel Sánchez

Associate Dean, Fish School
Director, Scarborough Institute of Church Planting & Growth
Professor of Missions
Southwestern Baptist Theological Seminary, Fort Worth, TX 76122

Somebody once said, "If those folks are heretics who argue that every saved believer will attain sinless perfection on earth (and they are), worse heretics are all of us who are satisfied with sinful imperfection." I feel a parallel statement is true about the subject Dr. Ebbie Smith addresses very effectively in his book, *Only Jesus: Jesus Christ the One and Only Savior.*

Dr. Smith makes the strong case from the biblical perspective that people can be saved only by coming to know Jesus Christ as Savior and Lord. Thus, it is heresy to teach / preach universalism or inclusiveness that would suggest other ways exist for one to be made right with God apart from trusting in Jesus. It is also practical heresy to believe this truth and still refuse to inform others about the only way to God.

Dr. Smith's work is a fine addition to the effort to witness clearly to Jesus as only Savior and Lord as God's only begotten. The attractiveness of universalism to those who have lost friends and loved ones makes truth concerning this subject even more vital and timely.

Dr. Clyde Glazener

Pastor
Gambrell Street Baptist Church
1616 W. Gambrell Street
Fort Worth, Texas 76115

Only Jesus

*Jesus Christ The One
and Only Savior*

Ebbie C. Smith

Church Starting Network
2012

Only Jesus
Jesus Christ the One
and Only Savior

Library of Congress Cataloging-in-Publication Data

Ebbie C. Smith 1932--

ISBN 978-0-9852842-0-6

Printed and bound in United States of America

Dedication

To all who are striving to communicate the message
of "Only Jesus" to the multitudes in the World
today who have yet to find Eternal Life that
comes exclusively through faith in the one and only
Living Savior, Christ Jesus.

Contents

Foreword

Roy J. Fish

Encroaching relativism and smothering tolerance have become dominate attitudes in our world today. In such a deadening atmosphere, it is refreshing to read a book that expresses definite and clearly understood convictions. Such a book is Ebbie C. Smith's, *Only Jesus: Jesus Christ The One and Only Savior*. Smith clearly states his basic conviction that ". . . the only promise we have of salvation is *in Jesus Christ and one's faith encounter with him during one's lifetime*. Jesus alone is Savior; Jesus is the one and only Savior" (p. v). This promise, says Smith, is the only biblical assurance of eternal life.

Smith clearly presents and rejects the teachings of the "wider-hope theorists"—Universalism, Pluralism, and Inclusivism. He demonstrates that these teachings simply are not congruent with biblical truth. This book firmly indicates that the Bible does not support the teachings of:

- All people finally coming to salvation,
- Conditionalism (Annihilationism),
- Post-mortem decision,
- Salvation in any other religion
- Views of Hell as retributive, cleaning, and temporary

Only Jesus: Jesus Christ The One and Only Savior finds no promise for salvation other than one's personal experience with the Christ.

This book does not question the power of God to save persons in any way the Lord chooses. In fact, the author admits he would feel more comfortable if he could hold some of the "wider-hope" teachings. It is not the spirit of the teachings that Smith rejects but their accuracy and conformity to biblical doctrine.

What this book does conclude is, however, that if any way of salvation other than explicit faith and commitment to Jesus Christ exists, the Bible is totally silent on it. Humanity has, says Smith, no promise of salvation except by this faith. We cannot, therefore, rely on any other way of salvation nor can we promise to others any alternate possibility. We might feel more comfortable in believing in other ways of salvation but we must rely solely on the totally accurate revelation of the Bible, the perfect and errorless guide to belief and practice.

One emphasis in the book that is not always heard relates to the joy and blessing of salvation in life. Walking with Jesus is the most rewarding and joyous life possible. Any who fail to receive new life in Christ not only miss eternal life in Heaven and its joys but also the great blessing of living with him during lifetime.

The primary point of *Only Jesus: The One and Only Savior* goes beyond clarifying the confusion of the "wider-hope" theories. These theories certainly are not based on Scripture and Evangelicals must turn from them. Smith's concern is, however, far less on the error of these confused theologians and writers but on the neglect and failure of more theologically correct persons who are often limited and negligent in the proclamation of the message of the loving Lord who alone promises eternal life. He writes:

> I am concerned about people named Rahner, Talbot, Pinnock, Sanders, Ferré, Hicks, and Robertson who hold to wider-hope theories. I am, however, far more and more deeply concerned about those of us who accept the biblical truth of Only Jesus yet do so little about sharing this message with the lost. *Is it not possible that our negligence in effective witness is the greatest liberalism of all?* (p. 159).

We need to hear Smith on the biblical errors in the views of the "wider-hope" writers. We need even more to heed his call to increased faithfulness in the great task of sharing the Good News of Jesus to all people in every land. Please read this book. Read the book but please react in renewed and more faithful witness.

We have here a book that moves against the currents of much current thinking. Let us allow this book to bring balance into the Christian thinking of our day. Let us follow the urging of this book and expand our efforts in evangelism and missions in every corner of this globe.

Roy J. Fish

Distinguished Professor Emeritus of Evangelism and Former L.R. Scarborough Chair of Fire Southwestern Baptist Theological Seminary, Ft. Worth, Texas

Preface

This book could easily have been much larger. The subjects covered are vast, imperative, and vital. I deliberately limited the number of pages to make it more readable and hopefully more widely read.

My emphasis is not on an in-depth presentation of the materials but on the imperative necessity of effective evangelism. I seek to address Christians who should be actively engaged in the all-consuming effort to spread the Message of Jesus Christ, the one and only Savior, to people and peoples around the world.

The central conviction addressed in this study relates to how people find salvation in Jesus Christ. At the center of this study rests the belief of "Only Jesus," that is, the only promise we have of salvation is *in Jesus Christ and one's faith encounter with him during one's lifetime*. Jesus *alone* is Savior; Jesus is the *only* Savior.

A second and equally valid conviction, "Jesus Only," expresses *the belief that we need not, indeed must not, add anything to Jesus*. Church membership, baptism, good works, and faithful service hold vast importance for the Christian life. None of these is, however, essential for salvation. *This imperative question will comprise the subject for a later study*.

We understand and hold faithfully to the teachings of Jesus is the one, only, and sufficient Savior. We accept this statement as truth. Holding firmly to this belief, *we must live by and act on* our understanding of this biblical truth.

We might, however, hold this teaching without wavering, defend it tenaciously, and yet do little or nothing to help the staggering millions who are outside God's salvation. Under such conditions, we have:

- Accomplished nothing
- Proven ourselves unfaithful to our Lord
- and indeed remain under God's judging eye.

Doctrinal orthodoxy, while of immense importance, becomes little more than rhetoric when it does not result in praxis, the activity of actually sharing the Good News with people everywhere (including across the street). *This book reaches its purpose only as it stimulates believers everywhere to participate directly and personally in his great and imperative mission of worldwide evangelism.*

Please allow the following words to guide you in an understanding of the biblical teachings on salvation and how this blessed state comes to people through the grace of Almighty God. I hope you can see through the wider-hope promises and maintain your convictions of Only Jesus. My urgent prayer is, however, that we never substitute biblical convictions for loving service. These two efforts, believing and acting, must work in unison and cooperation. Believing without reservation that Christ is the only Savior we share him openly and without reservation with peoples everywhere.

Ebbie C. Smith
Fort Worth, Texas
February 2012

CHAPTER 1

TWO PRESSING QUESTIONS

Two pressing and provocative questions face Christians in the 21st century. Both questions find expression in the statement, *Only Jesus, Jesus Only*. The first of these demanding questions concerns the query, "Does salvation reside in *any* source other than Jesus Christ?" and addresses what we mean by "Only Jesus."

The second question considers the concept of, "Is there *anything* other than personal faith in Christ that must be added in seeking God's Salvation?" This question addresses the meaning of "Jesus Only."

Effective Christian witnesses must face, consider, and answer these two burning questions.

Two Pressing Questions

1. Is Christian Salvation available from any source (religion or program) other than personal faith in the Historic Jesus, the Christ?

2. Is simple faith in the Lord Jesus Christ sufficient for Christian Salvation or must it be supplemented by some addition?

The First Question

The viewpoint, Only Jesus, considers several pressing matters.

The Unquestioned Uniqueness Of Jesus Christ

The central issue in understanding the biblical basis of and motivation for Christian theology and missions is the uniqueness of Christ and the Gospel as revealed in the Bible. This truth remains unquestioned and unquestionable for

Evangelical believers. Contemporary discussions of religions, however, increasingly question this basic teaching of biblical Christianity. Questioning of Christ's uniqueness and therefore the uniqueness of Christianity stem from without (the other religions and the non-religious) and also from the inside (those who see salvation from sources other than Christ). Herbert Kane declares that "In a pluralistic world it is becoming increasingly difficult to maintain the uniqueness of the Christian faith" (1982:105). Kane continues asserting that to the non-Christian peoples the teachings of exclusiveness is the most offensive aspect of contemporary Christianity (Ibid.).

The Relationship of Christianity and the Religions

In dealing with the first of these questions contemporary Christian witnesses must also consider the relationship between Christianity and the religions and cults of humankind. Theologians call this study, *theologia religionum*"or "A Theology of Religions" (Bosch 1991:477; Copeland 1999: vii). Lalsangkima Pachuau points out that a "theology of religions" is different from a "theology of religion" (2000:553).

The theology of religion seeks to explain what religion is and interpret the universal religious experiences of humankind. A theology of religions, on the other hand, studies the various religious traditions from the standpoint of the history of salvation and the various approaches to the mystery of Jesus Christ and the Christian Church (Ibid, 553). A "theology of religions" addresses the questions of revelation in and salvation through the religions and Christianity's claim to uniqueness, that is, the claim that Christianity alone provides salvation (Smith 1998: 416).

David Bosch declares that the problem of a theology of religions presents the Christian Church with an "unprecedented challenge." The Christian movement has, he writes, reached a point where without doubt the two largest unsolved problems are Christianity's relationship to the world religions which offer this-worldly salvation and to the other faiths (1991:476-77). Lalsangkima Pachuau declares that the question of salvation in religions other than the faith in Jesus Christ is the hub of missionary theology (2000:555). J.

2

Verkuyl insists that while the relationship of Christianity to other religions has been in place from the beginning of the Christian faith, that the present day marks a time for "fresh thinking" related to this subject (1978:341). Harold Netland declares that no other issue so clearly illustrates current theological and missiological ferment than the question of the relation between Christian faith and the other religious traditions (1995:3).

The study of a theology of religions occupies an increasingly prominent place in Christian writings. Interpreters fall into two basic camps. Some believe that *only* a saving relationship with Jesus Christ during one's lifetime provides salvation or eternal life and are known as Exclusivists, Particularists, or Replacement theologians.

Other interpreters, called Universalists, Pluralists, or Inclusivists, hold some form of "wider-hope" theory. Wider-hope theories teach that salvation is accessible in a way or ways other than this unique relationship with Christ during lifetime. Followers of these views make up a constantly expanding and increasingly vocal section of contemporary theologians.

Universalists believe that all people will eventually come to God's salvation. Pluralists contend that salvation can be found in many approaches or religions. Inclusivists hold that salvation is only in Christ but are certain that Christ can be found in many religions and or general revelation. Obviously these writers see some means other than personal relationship with Christ by repentance and faith during a person's lifetime.

Many differences in viewpoint exist within these wider-hope groups.[*] In fact, writers often place the same people in different groupings. For example, John Hick is sometimes called a Universalist while at other times he is considered a Pluralist or even an inclusivist (Parry and Partridge 2003: xvii-xviii; Sanders 1992). Universalists, pluralists, and inclusivists, however, are organized in this book as wider-hope theories or approaches that see salvation in ways other than

---

[*]A fourth model is sometimes added to the primary three of Exclusivism, Inclusivism, and Pluralism and that is what Paul Knitter calls the Acceptance Model that is seen in the views of Postmodernism, the Liberalist approach of George Lindbeck, or the multiple salvations taught by Mark Heim.

simple faith in Jesus Christ.

Many writers do not include Universalism among the wider-hope alternatives. This view that all will be eventually saved and united with God does, however, contend that salvation is not limited to those who come into a direct personal relationship with Christ during that person's lifetime. Universalists tend to uphold a second chance after death and deny the eternal nature of Hell. By its nature, universal salvation constitutes a wider-hope approach that is not in line with the biblical teaching of *Only Jesus.*

Theologians and religious interpreters continue discussing the approaches of wider-hope theories and particularist views in various types of writings. A short and therefore limited article on the overall subject appears in James F. Lewis and William G. Travis *Religious Traditions of the World*, Part V "Contemporary Theologies Of Religion," Zondervan, 1991:355-404. Another brief treatment of the subject is Ebbie C. Smith, "Contemporary Theology of Religions," in *Missiology: An Introduction to the Foundations, History, and Strategies of World Missions*, ed. John Mark Terry, Ebbie Smith, and Justice Anderson (Broadman & Holman, 1998: 416-33). J. Verkyul, in his one chapter discussion of the theologies of religions, delves deeply into the teachings of various theologians and approaches and provides an indispensable discussion of the subject of a theology of religions (1978:341-72). The brevity of these articles hold them to limited overviews of the subject.

Other works summarize the debate by dedicating an entire book to the subject of a theology of religions. Ronald H. Nash, *Is Jesus the Only Savior?* (Zondervan, 1994) approaches the study of a theology of religions from a firm exclusivist position. John Sanders, on the other hand, in *No Other Name: An Investigation into the Destiny of the Unevangelized* (Eerdmans 1992), considers the subject from a more inclusivist viewpoint.

E. Luther Copeland, *A New Meeting of the Religions* (Baylor University Press, 1999) studies the theology of religions from a moderately exclusivist position. From a different persuasion, Paul Knitter continues his insistence on "wider-hope" views. Knitter adds to his earlier book, *No Other Name?* (1985) by tracing the various theological positions and adding his own and a new organization in *Introducing Theologies of Religions* (2005).

Other works provide discussions or debates between proponents of the various sides of the issue. Dennis L. Okholm & Timothy Phillips, eds. *More than One Way?: Four Views on Salvation in a Pluralistic World* (Zondervan 1995) bring together proponents of various views in joint discussion of the issues. This helpful volume was published in 1996 under the title, *Four Views on Salvation in a Pluralistic World*.

John Sanders edited *What About Those Who Have Never Heard?* (1995). He brings together Gabriel Fackre, himself, and Ronald Nash to discuss contrasting views of Divine Perseverance, Inclusivism, and Restrictivism. Each participant critiques the words of the others.

Still other books provide an overview of the entire field of a theology of religions. Veli-Matti Kärkkäinen provides a comprehensive and deeply theological work on the overall subject of theology of religions that explains most of the divergent viewpoints in, *An Introduction to the Theology of Religions: Biblical, Historical, and Contemporary Perspectives* (2003). Attention has already been directed to Paul Knitter's book *Introducing Theologies of Religion*.

Over against the approaches that visualize some wider-hope, the approach of exclusivism (particularism) *holds that only implicit faith in the historical Jesus during a person's lifetime can lead to salvation in the biblical sense*. Particularism holds that Jesus alone is Savior and that this salvation is found only in a faith relationship with the Christ.

The exclusivist position does not rest on pride or feelings of superiority but only on its belief that this view is the direct teachings of Scripture. Exclusivism speaks not of the superiority of Christianity over other systems but rather of the uniqueness of the Person and work of Jesus Christ (Van Engen 1995: 187-92; Ott, Strauss, and Tennent 2010: 318). Particularists stand firmly on the promise of John 20:31 (Nichols 1994:11-12).

The Exclusivist view has been the basic Christian teaching over most of history. Some wider-hope thinking emerged in early Christian thinkers. The question does not, however, in any way constitute a matter of history. The important aspect of this question regards faithfulness to biblical teachings.

The possibility or impossibility of salvation in religions other than Christianity is far more than a theological exercise. The question has deep implications for ministry, theology, and missions. Discussions of the question of exclusivism in the Particularist view and the views of wider-hope theories consume many writers and vast amounts of literature in contemporary libraries.

Inclusivist, Clark Pinnock declares the question of Christianity's uniqueness, "one of the hottest topics on the agenda of theology in the nineties" (1992:7). John Cobb declares this area of study to be "a burning Issue" (2002:2). Rob Bell declares that the teachings of Exclusivism call out disturbing questions about the belief itself, the faith of those who hold it, and the kind of God related to the teaching (2011:3).

Harold Netland affirms that the questions surrounding Christianity and the religions clearly illustrate the "current theological ferment" (1995:3). Gerald Anderson declares that no issue in missiology holds more importance, raises more controversy, or provides more diversity than matters related to the relationship between Christianity and the religions. Anderson names the question of Christianity and the religions as "the" theological issue for the 1990s and into the 21st century (1993:200-201). Particularist, James Leo Garrett Jr., refers to this subject as an "increasing controversy" (2000:1:661).

The issue represents one of the most crucial challenges to Christian theology since the danger and opportunity posed by Darwinism, according to E. Luther Copeland (1999:7). Eric Sharpe believes the challenges of the teachings of salvation in other religions to be a more serious challenge to Christianity than any secular attack and calls the questions of a theology of religions "the epitome of mission theology" (1974:14). This book tries to guide readers in considering the seemingly unanswerable questions about a Christian theology of religions approach to the study.

Taxonomies of Approaches

Many approaches to the theology of religions seek to construct a taxonomy or classification of views. A brief view of these attempts shows the near impossibility of a consensus on the question of any taxonomy of views. Contemporary writers criticize and rework Alan Race's well-known classification of pluralism, inclusivism, and exclusivism. Amos Yong declares that the three-fold taxonomy may have outlived its usefulness. He further states that the traditional categories are becoming ". . . murky through a variety of qualifications" (2003:28).

Race's categories remain, however, a basic approach to the teachings concerning salvation in Christ only or salvation in other religions as well. Questioners of the division have done little to replace it. Race's three-fold taxonomy of theologies of religion has been called "the Classic Paradigm" (Ott, Strauss, Tennent 2010:293).

While some variation in the statement of the viewpoint is evident, most taxonomies in some way form a restatement of Race's arrangement. A diagram of Race's view follows:

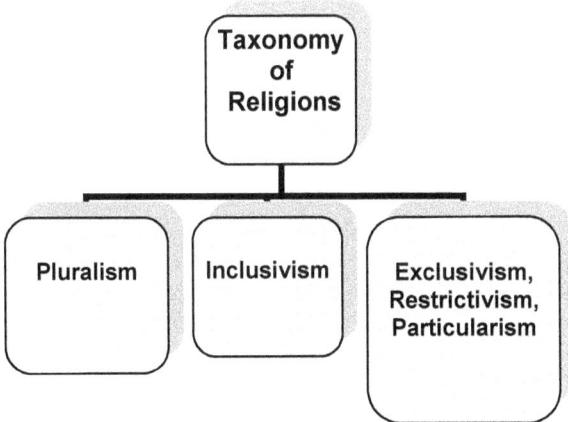

Paul F. Knitter, from his decided wider-hope stance, suggests an adapted model for theologies of religions. He uses the concepts of the Replacement Model, the Fulfillment Model, The Mutuality Model, and The Acceptance Model.

The total replacement model equates to the exclusivist or

particularistic approach. He remarks that the views of exclusivism consider that Christianity replaces all non-Christian religions. Knitter is correct in that Exclusivists hold firmly to the teaching that Christ is the one true revelation of God and is *the* light not *just one of* the lights and the people who are without Christ are without hope (Eph 2:12) (2002:19-32). C. Gordon Olson speaks of the uniqueness of Christ and sums up the discussion of this viewpoint with the term, "the only light in the deadly night" (1998:65-79).

Further, exclusivists contend that faith is centered on the proclamation of the historical death and resurrection of Christ. They are convinced that salvation comes only through repentance and faith in Christ's death on the cross and that no one can be saved apart from the knowledge of Christ. Scriptures such as John 14:6, 1 John 5:1-12; John 3:16-18, 36 are central to the thinking of exclusivism.

Hendrick Kraemer expressed the exclusivist position in his acclaimed book, *the Christian Message in a Non-Christian World.* Kraemer championed what he called "radical discontinuity" between Christianity and the religions. He questioned the validity of general revelation and held strongly to the position that only in Christ was salvation possible (see Kraemer 1938).

The exclusivist position is not, however, monolithic. Knitter's taxonomy suggests a Partial Replacement Model that relates to Bible-based Christians he calls "New Evangelicals." These exclusivists, says Knitter, are more open to general revelation as a revelation from God and as pathways or conduits to God rather than obstacles to God's presence. They see no salvation in the religions but do believe that God provides truth about himself and that people have been able to assess some truth through general revelation.

These truths in other religions can provide points of continuity when they are congruent with biblical teachings. Knitter clarifies, however, that exclusivists, either of the total or partial replacement persuasion, teach that one can only be saved as they come into an explicit contact with Jesus and his Gospel. Knitter places writers like Harold Netland in the partial replacement school (2002:33-49).

Knitter expresses his unique wider-hope philosophy in his

edited work, *The Myth of Christian Superiority* (2005). He directly states that his use of the teachings of Buddha helped him to find deeper faith in Jesus (2009). In the preface to his 2005 work, Knitter expresses his hope that the wider-hope thinking will be more widely accepted. He declares that his book sounds two bells (1) an alarm bell and an invitation bell. The alarm, he says, seeks to alert Christians (but not only Christians) to the pressing need to take other religious more seriously, to get to know them, talk with them, and work with them. The invitation bell intends to show the exciting, life-giving, world-benefiting, faith-deepening benefits that result from engaging and learning about persons who follow other religious ways. Knitter believes that in our present age, religious people have be religious interreligiously and that to walk one's own faith-path, one must be walking with others from different paths (2005:xi).

Knitter's taxonomy can be diagramed:

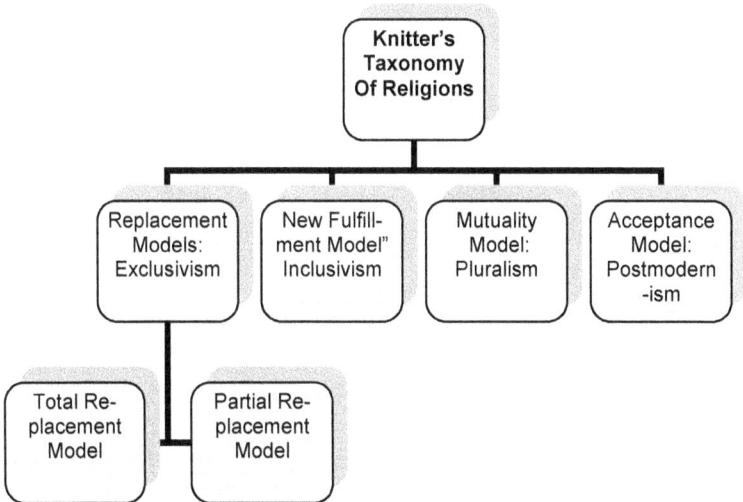

One major contribution in Knitter's new attempt at a taxonomy of the religions is his addition of the fourth category, The Acceptance Model," which Knitter describes as teaching, "many true religions: so be it" (2002:171). The Acceptance Model, according to Knitter, finds its expressions in postmodernism, the postliberalism of persons such as George Lindbeck, and the multiple salvations seen in Mark Heim's writings (Knitter 2002: 173-91; See Ott, Strauss, Tennent

2010: 294).

Charles VanEngen also seeks to modify the taxonomy of Race. Clearly from an Evangel stance, VanEngen suggests a fourth category he calls "An Evangelistic Paradigm." This view seeks to place the concept of Jesus is Lord at the center of Christian teaching and practice. Salvation is much more than joining the Christian religion (certainly than accepting any Christian Church). Salvation is finding a personal relationship with the eternal God through a living relationship with Jesus Christ. The Evangelistic Paradigm, says VanEngen, corrects the triumphalism and arrogance of many Exclusivists. This view places emphasis on the Kingdom of God rather than the Church. The approach is both culturally pluralistic, ecclesiologically inclusivist, and faith particularist (1995: 184-201). VanEngen's approach is filled with truth and contributes much but remains basically a particularist version of the taxonomy of religions.

Daniel Strange has proposed a different taxonomy of religions in *The Possibility of Salvation Among the Unevangelized: Analysis of Inclusivism in Recent Evangelical Theology.* Christopher Morgan calls this book, "arguably the best work by an exclusivist to date" (2008:21).

Strange organizes the views of salvation for the unevangelized in two major divisions that actually become nine categories (2001:304-331). This taxonomy immediately divides the viewpoints into those that teach particular accessibility and those that teach universal accessibility (2001:307 and 321). He places six groups under particular accessibility and three in the group of universal accessibility.

Daniel Strange has developed a most promising discussion to the various approaches to a taxonomy of the religions.

Strange's view is diagramed:

```
                 ┌─────────────────────────┐
                 │   Taxonomy of Religions  │
                 │      Daniel Strange      │
                 └─────────────────────────┘
              ┌──────────────┐    ┌──────────────┐
              │  Particular  │    │  Universal   │
              │ Accessibility│    │ Accessibility│
              └──────────────┘    └──────────────┘
```

Hard Restrictivism Carl Henry	Agnostic Restrictivism Okholm and Philipps	**Post mortem Opportunity G. Franke**
Soft Restrictivism Shedd	*Preparatio Evangelica* Piper	Middle Knowledge Craig
Opaque Exclusivism Heim	Non-Reformed Exclusivism	Positive Agnosticism Stott

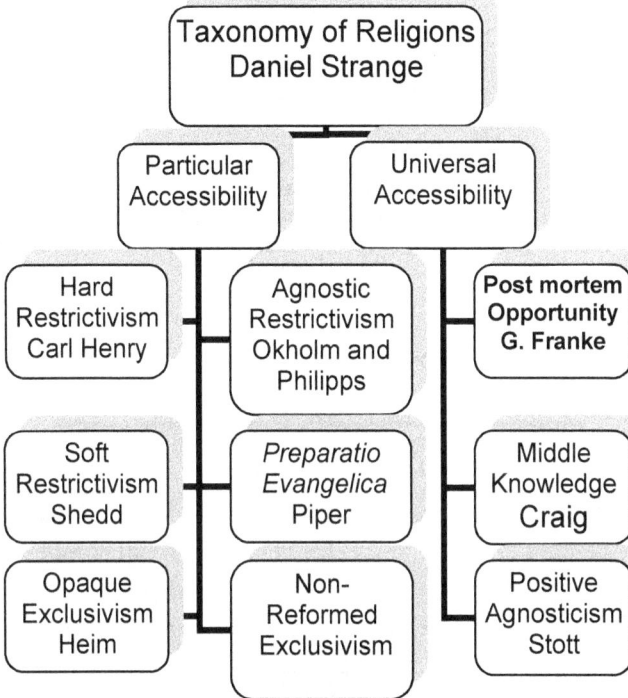

Strange's taxonomy certainly provides material for thought and deeper understanding of the various approaches to a theology of religions. The approach does not, however, include all the writers and indicate where they would be placed. For example, where would Ronald Nash and Harold Lindsell be placed? Persons such as Pinnock and Sanders are not on the taxonomy and indeed one is uncertain as to which category they might fit. Moreover, Alister McGrath has no place in Strange's categories but seems to be given a category separate and distinct from the taxonomy.

Still, one interested in the subject of a theology of religions should consider the work of Daniel Strange. We would accept the judgment of Christopher Morgan that this book is one of the better works on the subject.

A new and improved proposal for taxonomy of the Religions by Craig Ott, Stephen J. Strauss with Timothy C. Tennent sets out a proposed nomenclature for Theology of Religions. This suggestion basically eliminates Knitter's "Partial Replacement" model and uses the term "Revelatory Particularism" to express the views usually called Exclusivism.

Only Jesus

This new model expresses Inclusivism as Universal Inclusivism, Pluralism as dialogic Pluralism, and the Acceptance Model as Narrative Postmodernism. This interesting approach can be diagramed:

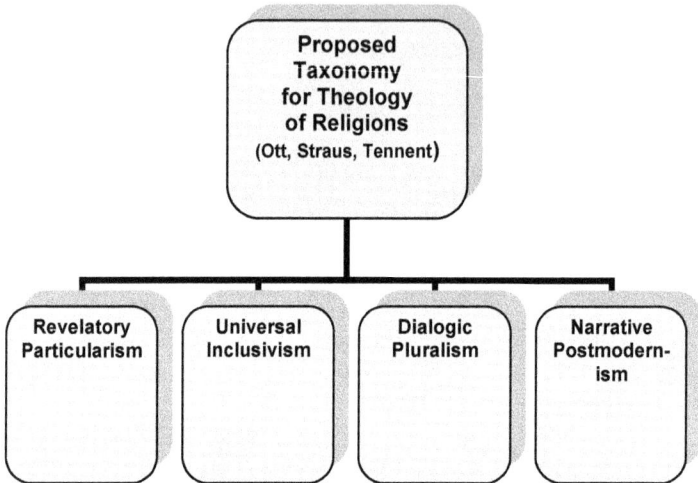

```
                    ┌─────────────────────┐
                    │     Proposed        │
                    │     Taxonomy        │
                    │   for Theology      │
                    │   of Religions      │
                    │ (Ott, Straus, Tennent) │
                    └─────────────────────┘
                              │
        ┌──────────┬──────────┼──────────┬──────────┐
  ┌───────────┐ ┌───────────┐ ┌───────────┐ ┌───────────┐
  │ Revelatory│ │ Universal │ │ Dialogic  │ │ Narrative │
  │Particularism│ │Inclusivism│ │ Pluralism │ │Postmodern-│
  │           │ │           │ │           │ │    ism    │
  └───────────┘ └───────────┘ └───────────┘ └───────────┘
```

The organization of Ott, Strauss, and Tennent contributes much to the discussion of Theologies of Religion. These scholars correctly point out that the term "revelatory" expresses the importance of revelation in Scripture and in Jesus Christ. Further, the word, "particularism" is, they contend, more precise than exclusive (2010:312). The foundations of this approach are sound.

While agreeing with the basic concepts of the new organization above, this book continues to use the terminology of Exclusive, Inclusive, and Pluralist for purposes of communication. We will, however, employ as needed and helpful for clarification, the more useful and recent terminologies.

Both the critics of Race's classification and the creators of new taxonomies, however, usually consist of little more than a restatement or expansion of Race's categories. Problems exist with every classification. The problems of those approaches that seek to deviate from Race's traditional approach are clearly seen in Knitter's classification. The various approaches overlap and shade into one another.

Ronald Nash slices to the heart of the issue, asking, "Is

Jesus the Only Savior?" In current theology Nash recognizes three different answers, "No,"; "Yes, but . . ."; and "Yes, period" that conform to the traditional categories. Nash actually sees validity in only the exclusivist (restrictivist, particularist) position (1994:9). This book agrees in principle with the approach of Nash.

I suggest only three major categories (with the acceptance model acknowledged but not actually considered in this approach). The Pluralist, Inclusivist, and Universalistic positions I place under the one category, Wider-hope views.

- The wider-hope theories (placing universalism among the wider-hope approaches)

- The exclusivist position holds firmly that Jesus Christ is the one and only Savior

- The Acceptance Model that basically says the difference is present but of little consequence (see Knitter 2005:171-191).

This study does not accept the teachings of the "wider-hope approaches" nor the Acceptance Model. The universalistic concept does not square with biblical doctrines; the pluralists and inclusivist approaches fall short of biblical accuracy. This book holds the Exclusivist (Particularist) position and contends that, S*alvation can be attained only through a person's direct faith response, during his/her lifetime, to the message and person of the Historic, Risen Christ as presented in the Christian Gospel.*

The author of this book considers Universalism but another wider-hope theory. Certainly, striking differences exist between Universalism and the other wider-hope approaches but in essence, Universalism opts for more opportunities for attaining salvation than faith in Christ during lifetime. Exclusivism agrees with the spirit of desiring to find more opportunities for people to come to salvation. The followers of Particularism cannot, however, find support for the wider-hope ideas in Scripture. The only certain promise we have is the biblical assurance that those who believe, that is, trust themselves to the love of God in Christ Jesus, will have eternal life. Without questioning or doubting the teaching, this book proclaims that the Bible teaches that Jesus Christ is the *one and only Savior* and that salvation is found only in an explicit faith relationship with God in Christ during the believer's lifetime.

The position of this book can be diagramed:

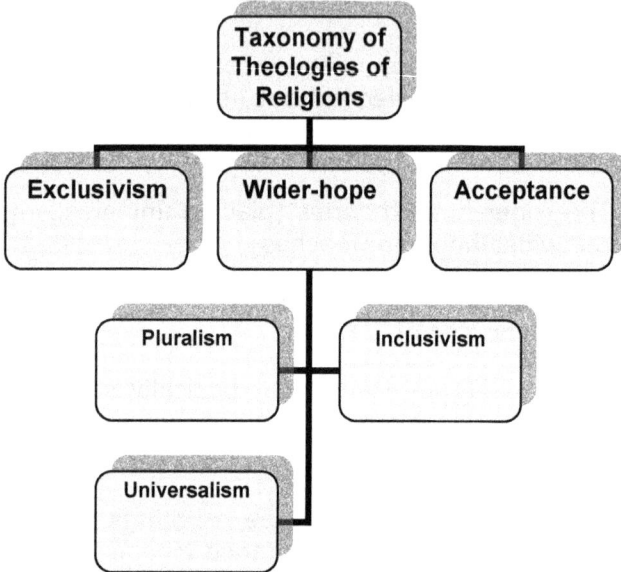

```
                    ┌─────────────────┐
                    │  Taxonomy of    │
                    │  Theologies of  │
                    │  Religions      │
                    └─────────────────┘
        ┌───────────────────┼───────────────────┐
  ┌──────────────┐   ┌──────────────┐   ┌──────────────┐
  │ Exclusivism  │   │  Wider-hope  │   │  Acceptance  │
  └──────────────┘   └──────────────┘   └──────────────┘
                          │
              ┌───────────┴───────────┐
        ┌──────────────┐       ┌──────────────┐
        │  Pluralism   │       │ Inclusivism  │
        └──────────────┘       └──────────────┘
              │
        ┌──────────────┐
        │ Universalism │
        └──────────────┘
```

This question concerning the possibility of salvation in religions other than faith in Jesus Christ is worthy of full attention by all Christians. A lessening of the conviction involved in the expression, "Only Jesus" is all too obvious in contemporary writings. The current debate on this issue demands that Christians everywhere take it into full consideration.

The second and equally important question suggested in this book which will be addressed directly in a future study, relates to the tendencies to add something to the message of simple faith in Christ. Various groups have persisted in efforts to add some requirement, always manmade, to the simple message of faith in Christ.

The Second Question

The second critical question is no less important to faithful witnesses than the first. This question inquires about teachings that seek to add something other than faith in Christ to the plan of salvation. Through Christian history the tendency has arisen whereby various teachers have sought to add to the concept of *only Jesus*, that is, that Jesus alone is sufficient for salvation and that no additional aspects should be attached.

This second important question will be the subject for a future study. Efforts to place both questions in one study have convinced the writer that such arrangements would cloud more than clarify. We encourage readers to keep both questions in mind as they consider the implications of both inquiries.

Only Jesus

CHAPTER 2

THE UNIVERSALISTIC
APPROACH

Gregory MacDonald declares that "At the most simple level Christian univeralism is the belief that God will (or, in the case of "hopeful universalism," might) redeem all people through the saving work of Christ" (2011: 1). This view, that all humanity will eventually be saved and come into proper relationship with God, is at heart a wider-hope approach. Universalists project salvation for every person, whether or not they hear and respond to the Gospel, or regardless of how evil they might be or have been. Access to salvation does not, according to Universalism, depend on if they really want this salivation. In the end, the love of God will overcome all rebellion and bring every person to proper relationship with him. Speaking with typical universalistic optimism, Richard Trudeau strongly contends that "Somehow, God finds a way to save *everybody*" (2009:18).

In a careful critique and rejection of the beliefs of Universalists, J. I. Packer reminds readers that the salvation of all people would include those who have held the most serious errors in beliefs and engaged in the most disturbing of practices. He shows that Universalism asserts the final salvation of such unsavory characters as Judas, Adolf Hitler, Genghis Khan, Stalin, and Saddam Hussein (2004a: 170-71). The truth of Packer's critique can be plainly seen in the contention of some Universalists that Satan and the demons will be brought to God (Talbott 1999:167, 197).

In answer, Universalists point to belief in a loving and sovereign God, who cannot and will not allow any to be forever lost. They believe that eternal separation in Hell is an unjust, too severe punishment for a finite sin of rejecting God (Pinnock 1992:156-57, 168-69; Talbott 1999:39; 2003:3-13). The theologian Friedrich Schleiermacher contended that if eternal damnation existed, then eternal bliss could not since the awareness of suffering in Hell would destroy the blessedness of those in Heaven (1928:721).

Universalism obviously totally rejects the basic proposition of "Only Jesus." In essence, Universalism finds a hope for salvation outside the biblically communicated revelation that promises this salvation only through a personal response to the historic Christ *during a person's lifetime.* The Universalistic doctrine that contends that the loving and all-powerful God will eventually bring all persons back to his loving presence finds expression in the writing of Philip Gulley and James Mulholland who declare that if one believes that God loves and will save every person, that person cannot claim redemption as exclusively Christian. Salvation cannot be, they say, the sole possession of a specific culture, religion, denomination, or person because Salvation belongs to God (2003: 124-25).

The final destiny or salvation of a person may not, say Universalists, be achieved until after that person's death. God's grace, they say, reaches beyond the grave. Timothy K. Beougher, who is not a Universalist, correctly observes that a shift can be seen in teachings of universalism from man who is too good for God to damn to God who is too good to damn man (1998:16, fn 6).

No straight-ticket approach exists among those who claim to be Universalists. Gregory MacDonald, in his *The Evangelical Universalist,* speaks of the "intellectual geography of Universalisms." He points to several types of Universalists and indicates he does not accept the views of some of these teachers.

One view of universalism, says MacDonald, teaches that the gospel message of Jesus is not intended for only one specific group of people. This view, certainly seen in the Bible, says MacDonald, teaches that God desires all people to be saved and that Jesus came to die for each and every person (2006, 2008:5). MacDonald believes the general teachings of Universalism go beyond this statement given by some who claim to be Universalists.

Some contemporaries hold even stronger views of universalism according to MacDonald. These Universalists contend that all people will be saved. Such versions often have differing views of the meaning of salvation and how people achieve it. MacDonald points to John Hick whom he calls a "pluralist Universalist." McDonald indicates that Hick believes that all people will be saved by God through whatever religious system he or she follows. Such a universalism, says

MacDonald, marginalizes Christ's role in salvation and deserves no serious attention (2006, 2008 5).

MacDonald shares his own type of universalism by introducing an imaginary representative he calls Anastasia. Anastasia, says MacDonald, believes in the crucial Christian doctrines such as the Trinity, creation, sin, atonement, the return of Christ, salvation through Christ alone, only by grace, and through nothing other than faith. She believes in the eschatological wrath of God, that is, Hell. Most, says MacDonald, would be hard pressed to tell her apart from other Evangelicals.

MacDonald affirms that Anastasia, the Universalist, differs from many Evangelicals in two primary beliefs. First, she is convinced that eternal destiny is not fixed at death. She believes that those in Hell can repent and seek God's forgiveness and mercy, that is, can be saved. A second belief is that in the end every person will seek God's salvation. This understanding is the type of universalism that Gregory MacDonald proposes (2006, 2008: 5-6).

Universalism gained an added thrust when in 1960-1961 the Universalist Church of America combined with the American Unitarian Association to form a new denomination often termed Unitarian Universalist Association (UUA). The name is often shortened to UU. The result is that today the UUA is a loose group dedicated to what is very near the social gospel.

The merger of Christian Universalism and Unitarianism was not and is not total. A decided difference exists between Christian Universalists and Unitarian Universalists. Unitarianism emphasizes freedom, reason, and tolerance. Christian Universalists hold strongly to beliefs in a Creator who desires relationship with all humans, that human souls can and do live on after physical death, that justice remains for people after death, and that all people will be eventually saved from sin and suffering (The Christian Universalist Association nd; 1).

Many Unitarians do not hold to these beliefs. Christian Universalism projects a spiritual message and claims that it is based on the 2000-year old history of Christian Universalism. Christian Universalism declares that it emphasizes in a more complete fashion the supreme worth of every human and the absolute universal nature of the love of God (Ibid).

Today Universalists teach and champion the concept of eventual salvation for all people (Trudeau 2009: 3-4). The option of accepting God's offer of salvation is, they contend, never removed (Reitan 2003:140). These statements clearly demonstrate the concept that Universalism is a wider-hope viewpoint and should take its place in the discussion of the wider-hope theories of salvation.

Overview of Universalism

Universalism can profitably be viewed from an overall perspective. Christian Universalism, also called *Universal Restoration* and *apokastastasis,* essentially contends that all human beings will finally be reconciled to God and that none will be forever lost (Ludlow 2000:38; Vincent 2005:5). Richard Trudeau declares that Universalism combines four "truths" or ideas:

- God is Love,

- No one is condemned,

- The way to be happy is to do good,

- There are sources of religious truth outside the Judeo-Christian tradition (2009:17).

These teachings obviously come under the general organization of a wider–hope theory of Salvation. Universalism projects a hope that goes beyond the simple faith in Christ during one's lifetime.

Most who follow Universalism do not, however, teach that salvation can be found other than in Christ. Universalism rather teaches that every person will be saved by Christ. Ken Allen writes that any true definition of Christian Universalism must include the belief that God is sovereign, loving, powerful, wise, just, and ultimately rules over everything. Allen says it must also include the conviction that salvation is only by faith in God and was finalized by Jesus Christ *"who gave Himself a ransom for all"* (1 Tim 2:6).

Some Universalists veer from the idea that all will be saved by God to a more pluralistic (see chapter 3) view that many paths lead to God. Universalists (especially those who have merged totally with Unitarians) project their belief in the "off centered cross." This symbol represents, they say, the universe with the empty space at the center showing the mystery at the heart of the universe that people call God.

The circle is drawn to represent the all-inclusive faith of universalism that shuts no one out. The off-centered cross shows that Christianity is an interpretation of infinity but *not the only* interpretation and not the necessary interpretation of all people (Trudeau 2009:10-12; Zeigler 1946: 558). This interpretation is not present in all expressions of Universalism. The view, however, obviously stamps many if not most Universalists as persons who add another path to salvation to the message of simple faith in Jesus Christ.

The basic definition of *Christian Universalism* includes the belief that God will save all persons. The view clings to the conviction that God is the one *truth"* (1 Tim 2:4) (Allen nd: 1). Universalism clearly does not accept nor agree with the basic tenant of *Only Jesus*.

Neil Punt provides a brief and comprehensive statement of the beliefs of universalism, writing that every person, without exception, will find salvation in Christ and that God's judgment against sin is temporary. Judgment against sin is designed to teach us to hate sin and flee to Christ for safety. Punt continues saying that all people will find salvation in Christ either in this life or in a future existence. (1980:2). Quillen Hamilton Shinn, in an early statement of the beliefs of universalism, affirms the movement's essence saying:

> The word Destiny distinguishes us [Universalists] from Christians of other churches. We believe in a good destiny for all. We believe God will make all his bad children good; he wants to, and he can. He has the disposition, the power, the means, and the time. If love is all conquering, there is no foe it will not subdue, not even the rebellious will of man (nd: 1).

Shinn continues that in addition to these four reasons that God will save all persons a million more reasons could be proposed (Ibid.)

Shinn calls his statements of the beliefs of universalism "Affirmations of Faith" (Nd: 1). In 1899, the General Convention of Universalists formulated brief statements of the "Five Essential Principles of the Universalist Faith" and the "Winchester Profession." These formulations contained the basic principles of Universalism:

- The Universal Fatherhood of God;

- The spiritual authority and leadership of His Son Jesus Christ;

- The trustworthiness of the Bible as containing a revelation from God;

- The certainty of just retribution for sin;

- The final harmony of all souls with God (Ken Allen nd.).

One Universalist, Mark Sanguinetti, sums up Universalist convictions declaring that Christian universalism is the belief of the desire and capabilities of Jesus Christ and that Jesus Christ came into the world to save all of mankind and not just a small percentage of the population. Sanguinetti teaches that Jesus not only had but still has the desire to save all people who have ever lived. God also, he contends, has the ability to save all people now and in the ages to come (2010:1).

Universalists do not, obviously, present a totally common front. In fact, one authority proclaims that "Only the belief that ultimately all men will be saved is common to all universalists" (Bauckham 1979:49). Universalists generally, however, reject ideas of eternal punishment, seeing punishment as redemptive rather than everlasting. The current popularity of some forms of universalism is, however, caught by Richard J. Bauckham who writes, ". . . . no traditional Christian doctrine has been so widely abandoned as that of eternal punishment" (1979:48). Albert Mohler adds the defenders of the belief in Hell are few since only "the most stalwart defenders of conservative theology retain it" (2004:16).

Brief History of Universalism

The history of Universalism is complex partially because this viewpoint is closely related to other difficult theological issues such as predestination and free will, the validity of retributive punishment, biblical authority, and the nature of God. Of particular concern in relation to the nature of God and universalism is the question of relation between the love of God and the justice of God.

Evangelical Christianity holds that most theological writers before the 19th century agreed with the teaching of eternal separation in Hell. These writers were, therefore, outside the viewpoints of Universalism. The voices that seemed to support a view of universalism mostly held concepts of annihilationism or some other form of conditional immorality. Eternal punishment was firmly declared in official creeds and confessions of Christianity and remained as much a part of Christian dogma as the doctrines of Trinity and Incarnation (Bauckham 1979:48).

Followers of Universalism, however, do not concur with the statement in the preceding paragraph. The teachings of universalism are not, according to Universalists, entirely a modern option. The theologian Origen in the Early Church period, says Universalist Ken R. Vincent, adopted the doctrine of Universal Restoration in which he taught that all people would be saved either immediately or eventually and all would go to Heaven (Vincent 2005: 3).

John Wesley Hanson declares that Origen wrote *Contra Celsum* in which he held to the view that human life was in stages leading to acceptance by God. Origen, whose views stemmed basically from Greek philosophy, thought that given unlimited time, God would draw all persons to himself, including Satan and the devils (See Origen, *Contra Celsum* 1965; and discussion of this idea in Mohler 2004: 17; Ramm 1964: 22 and Hanson 1899: 129-85).

Some Universalists contend that universalism was the prevailing dogma of the Christian Church during its first five hundred years (Hanson 1899:50). Hanson contends that the earliest Christian creeds and declarations of Christian opinion contain no statement of Christian belief in anything incompatible with the broad faith of the Gospel—the universal redemption of mankind from sin (1899:5).

Universalistic teaching contends that belief in an ever-lasting Hell and continuing separation from God stemmed from the teachings of Augustine (Talbott 1999:16). Speaking of Greek Christianity, Hanson declares that all the early statements of Christianity—*The Teaching of the Twelve Apostles, The Apostle's Creed,* and *The Nicene Creed* had no teaching of eternal punishment or separation. Teachings of universalism are obvious, according to Hanson, in the writings of such early theologians as Clement, Origen, The Gregories, Basil, the Great, Macrina, the Blessed, Theordore of Mopsuestia and many others. The Universalist movement with confidence claims that for almost 400 years the doctrinal statements of Christianity were entirely void of the lurid doctrine which after Augustine became the primary teaching of the Church for more than 1000 years (Hanson 1899:12-15, 188, 216, 306).

In one chapter Hanson calls the beginning of the doctrine of eternal punishment the "Deterioration of Christian Thought" (1899:260). He calls the change to teachings of eternal punishment the "great transition from the Christianity of the Apostles to the pseudo-Christianity of the patriarchs and emperors" and declares it began with Constantine. In fact, Hanson suggests that the doctrine of eternal Hell came from the Western adoption of teachings of heathenism. He writes:

> As the stones of the heathen temples were rebuilt into Christian churches, so the Pagan principles held by the masses modified and corrupted the religion of Christ; while the worldliness of secular interests derived from the union of church and state, exerted a debasing influence, and the Christianity of the Catacombs and of Origen became the church of the popes, of the Inquisition, and of the Middle Ages (1899:260).

Hanson insists that universal salvation remained the doctrine of Christendom so long as Greek, the language of the New Testament, was the language of Christianity. He taught that Universalism remained in Christian belief during the best centuries of the Church (the first three centuries) when the movement was most remarkable for simplicity, goodness, and missionary zeal. Universalism, he says, was least known when Greek was least known and Latin became the Church's language, during the church's darkest, most ignorant, and corrupt ages. Hanson's conclusion is:

> With the exception of the arguments of Augustine (A. D. 420), there is not an argument known to have been framed against Universalism for at least four hundred years after Christ, by any of the ancient fathers (1899:306).

Hanson's arguments (and those of other Universalists) are questionable. He does, however, raise an important point. If, as he says, universalism was accepted by the early Church why was not a voice raised against it? (Hanson 1899:16). According to Hanson, Although Justinian tried to eradicate universalism the doctrine was never totally replaced by teachings of eternal punishment. The views of Augustine did come to dominate the Christian faith in the subsequent history of Christianity (1899: 294-95).

Hanson's argument demands and deserves an answer. The doctrine of an eternal Hell was not well-developed among the Ante-Nicene Fathers but these leaders certainly projected the truth of the doctrine of eternal punishment. E. B. Pusey conclusively demonstrates that Origen's teachings denying eternal punishment were condemned and anathematized by the 5th General Council in 553 C.E. (1888:152-53). Further, Pusey quotes 84 patristic authors who spoke directly on Hell and most of whom left open the concept of endless punishment therein (1888: 139-290).

Augustine did not invent the teaching of an eternal Hell as a place of punishment. He did, however, contend that the biblical metaphors of fire and burning should be taken literally. The great theologian insisted that the punishments of Hell are eternal. Basing his conclusions on Matt 25:46, Augustine was convinced that if eternal life was endless and perpetual then so must be Hell and its terrors (1972: 1001-1002). In the main, Evangelicalism has followed the teachings of Augustine on the matter of eternal punishment in Hell and this teaching has become a strong motivation for the Christian mission.

Since 1800, the theological situation has changed drastically and Universalism retuned strongly upon the theological scene. Some writers who are not usually considered among Universalists question the concept of eternal punishment. Yet, a dominant voice supporting the doctrine of eternal punishment has sounded from mainline Christian teaching.

Movement toward universalism can be seen among 16-18th century writers. Historians see these movements as largely reaction to the particularisms of Calvinism. In the 19th century, theologian F. D. E. Schleiermacher became the first respected theological mind of modern times to support Universalism. Schleiermacher actually began from an almost Reformed position and ended with the belief that all were elected to salvation and the divine power would not fail.

Only a few theologians in the 19th century followed Schleiermacher. The views of these writers generally stemmed from aversion to the teachings of eternal punishment and Hell. Some of the 19th century Universalists actually based their convictions on the existence of conditional immortality and the idea of chances for salvation after death. Influence from evolutionary thinking also contributed to these moves toward Universalism.

In the 20th century, universalistic thinking turned more to the study of the texts about eternal punishment. Punishment was interpreted to be redemptive rather than eternally inflicting pain. These interpreters considered Hell a temporary torment from which sinners would finally emerge to salvation (Bauckham 1979:62). Universalists accepted the teaching that Hell involved punishment but considered the punishment as cleansing, remittable, and reforming. In fact, Thomas Talbott points out that they had no reason to reject the teachings of Hell as torment—since they believe it is as good a representation of God's purifying love as there is (1999:197-98).

Universalists in this period tended to base their arguments on biblical texts that they contended centered on the saving desire of God, the saving provision of God, and the saving promise of God (Beougher 1998: 9-11). During this period, some universalists considered the biblical warnings of eternal punishment to be only threats and not predictions. Most Universalists believe that to gain an acceptable teaching of the destiny of the unsaved, interpreters must go beyond the teachings of the New Testament (McDonald

2008:154-55). Universalists emphasize the love of God and center on passages that hold out a universal hope.

Some critics contend that Karl Barth and Emil Brunner had universalistic leanings. Oliver Crisp writes boldly:

> The scope of human salvation envisaged in the theology of Karl Barth is either a species of universalism, or comprises several distinct, incompatible strands of doctrine that he does not finally resolve (2011:322).

Barth categorically denies that he believes in Universalism in the well-known quotation concerning Universalism, "I do not teach it and I also do not teach it" (Jüngel 1986:477-78). Whatever the exact meaning of the quote is, Barth does separate himself from the teachings of Origin (CD II/2m 427, 477; CD IV/3: 476-78) (see Griggs 2007:196-2120). Crisp is convinced that Barth either moves to "necessary Universalism" or is inconsistent in his teachings (2011:322-23). Statements such as we have no theological rights to set any limits on God's loving kindness that is seen in Jesus Christ allow some writers to declare that Barth allowed universalism (Barth 1956;478; 1960:62). Such statements lead some to question Barth as to universalism and place him in a category of "hope-so" universalism (Beougher 1998:8-9; Núñez 1982:173).

A fair and thorough study of universalistic teachings would, however, place both Barth and Brunner outside the charge of being universalistic. Barth's doctrine of Election does show some leanings toward a type of Universalsim but in the main, Barth should not be considered a full-member of the Universalistic camp.

Dogmatic universalism finds, however, definite statement in numerous modern discussions. Nels Ferré, for example, advocates universalism based on his interpretation of God's *agape*. He believes the biblical material can be variously interpreted so as to deny the teachings of eternal damnation and reflect those of annihilation or universalism. The third of these alone, he says, is consistent with God's nature (Beougher 1998; 11). Ferré is convinced that God would violate his *agape* if he condemned any human to an eternal Hell (1963:24).

Only Jesus

Ferré confirms this belief as he writes:

> The logic of the situation is simple. Either God could not or would not save all. If He could not He is not sovereign; then not all things are possible with God. If He would not, again the New Testament is wrong, for it openly claims that He would have all to be saved (1947:24).

Ferré concludes that the New Testament message definitely projects a teaching that God both can and wants to save all. This statement is, says Ferré, "unanswerable" (1947; 118).

This theologian answers the question as to why the Bible says that some will be lost. Ferré answers in words that sound very much as if he is saying that the preaching of punishment is existential and not intended to be taken literally. He seems to be saying that God's word scares people with threats that God knows are untrue to gain a good end (1963:24). E.A. Blum sees this representation of the God of the Bible to be unworthy of the Father (1979:59).

Ferré, as his conclusion to the question of universalism, grieves that the doctrine of Hell could even come up in Christian thinking. That such a teaching could be conceived and believed shows, he says, how far from any understanding of God some people once were and alas, still are. To attribute eternal Hell to God is, according to Ferré, actually blasphemy and attributes the worst to the best (1951:228 and 1963:24). Hell must, according to Ferré, be seen as "having a door" (1951:241). This theologian obviously rests squarely in the Universalist camp.

Equally in the Universalist tradition, John A. T. Robinson bases his teaching on the conviction that only universal salvation is consistent with God's nature as omnipotent love. Universalism is not heretical, according to Robinson (1949:139-155). Final judgment and eternal separation would be an unthinkable frustration of God's purpose. Omnipotent love will in the end bring every person to yield to the Divine without any infringement of human freedom. The omnipotent love of God will elicit free choice from humans (See, Robinson 1949:140; Bauckham 1979:53-54; Beougher 1998:11).

Robinson does not dismiss the necessity of decision. He writes, "The blessed assurance of universalism, that, ultimately hell can be an actuality for none, in no way removes its relevance for decision" (1949:153). Two ways exist, according to Robinson. One way teaches that the road is crowded and leads to destruction. Those on the course of destruction will, however, eventually yield to the omnipotent Love itself. Robinson resorts to Origen's words that Christ remains on the Cross so long as one soul remains in hell. Universal salvation is embedded, says Robinson, in the necessity of God's nature (1949:155).

Robinson concludes his eloquent defense of universalism with these words:

> In a universe of love there can be no heaven which tolerates a chamber of horrors, no hell for any which does not at the same time make it hell for God. He cannot endure that—for *that* would be the final mockery of His nature—and He will not (1949:155).

Robinson is joined in his dogmatic universalism by John Hick. Hick, who is also discussed under the position of pluralism, follows basically the pattern of Robinson. He too sees two categories of passages in the New Testament—those that warn of separation and those that promise salvation. He contends, however, that no one will permanently refuse God's offer of eternal life. All will eventually repent (1976:247-49).

Hick is convinced that the evil and suffering in this world can only be justified if God brings to a good end every individual He has created. Should either eternal punishment or annihilation come to pass, then God would not be perfectly good. The traditional view of separation and punishment would mean, in Hick's thinking, either that God does not desire the salvation of some or that He is not omnipotent. Hick concludes that only universal salvation vindicates the omnipotent good God (1977: 341-45).

Universalism is certainly not a past movement. It continues to find expression. Rob Bell denies that he is a Universalist but in reality his book, *Love Wins*, expresses many of the conclusions of Universalism. Speaking of the teaching that separation will be a reality, Bell confidently states, "this

is misguided and toxic and ultimately subverts the conta-
gious spread of Jesus's message of love, peace, forgiveness,
and joy that our world desperately needs to hear" (2011:vii).
In later pages, Bell sounds the often heard argument of Universalists saying that eventually the love of God will melt the
hardest of hearts and bring all people to himself (2011:107).
God's love will in the end win all, says Bell (2011:109). Denny Burk says of Bell's book, "While Bell does not want to be
labeled a Universalist, this book does more to advance the
cause of universalism at the popular level than any book I
have ever seen" (2011:1).

Universalism is, obviously, alive and being taught in our
world. Evangelicals must hold firm to the biblical teachings of
separation from God and punishment for sin without taking
any joy in these messages. Evangelicals must say with John
Stott that as fashionable as universalism may be, it remains
incompatible with the teachings of Christ and His apostles
(1976:33).

In spite of the protestations of Universalist teachers, the
approach remains a deadly enemy of true evangelism. True
universalism, says Stott, is the call to universal evangelism
in obedience to Christ's universal commission. The biblical
teaching is not that all persons will be saved but that all
should hear the gospel of Christ's salvation in order that they
might believe and be saved (1976:33).

Every person concerned about and engaged in evangelism and discipleship must come to grips with the false hopes
of universalism. Although Universalists strive to avoid the
charge that the doctrine harms evangelistic thrust and passion, the charge remains a valid question. Harold Lindsell
affirms that Universalism cuts the nerve of missions and
evangelism   (1949: 153 and 229). Olson speaks of inclusivist thinking as ". . . very harmful in that it distorts Scripture
and seriously undermines the missionary program of the
church" (1998:66). Arthur Pierson, over a century ago, declared that a major reason Christianity allowed so many to
go without the gospel was the denial or at least doubt of
their lost condition (1886:291).

More recently, John Piper declares directly that a question about the lost condition will reduce the motivation for
missions. He points to three questions: "Will anyone experi-

ence eternal conscious torment under God's wrath?" "Is the work of Christ necessary for salvation?" "Is conscious faith in Christ necessary for salvation?"

Biblical answers to these three questions are crucial, says Piper, because in each case a negative answer diminishes the urgency of the missionary cause. There is a felt difference in the urgency when one believes that preaching the gospel is absolutely the only hope that anyone has of escaping the penalty of sin and forever in the happiness of God's presence (Piper 2010:kindle location 904). Piper concludes:

> So I affirm again that the abandonment of the universal necessity of hearing the gospel for salvation does indeed diminish the urgency of world evangelization. And I say again that   this is not the main reason for affirming the necessity of hearing and believing the gospel for salvation. The main reason is that the Bible teaches it, and therefore the good of man and the glory of God are most honored (Ibid).

Obviously, Evangelical Christianity and Universalism have vastly differing viewpoints on the possibility of Salvation outside of explicit, conscious faith in Christ. The Universalistic alternative is attractive and loving believers would be pleased to accept it. The Bible does not, however, have any teaching that will support the idea.

Basic Concepts of Universalism

As noted earlier, differences exist in the teachings of persons who follow what is called universalism. This variation is certainly apparent but students can identify a body of teaching that is basically shared by most of the followers of universalism. The following teachings are characteristic of those who follow the basic teachings of Universalism.

The following chart shows the basic concepts in Universalistic teachings concerning salvation, Heaven, and Hell.

BASIC CONCEPTS OF UNIVERSALISM

➢ Universalists insist that God is perfect love and will eventually reach all humans through his omnipotent love

➢ Universalists teach that Hell is temporary and corrective

➢ Universalists insist that early Christianity held to the doctrine of universal restoration and did not subscribe to the teachings of eternal punishment.

➢ Universalists insist they hold a high view of the value of humans.

➢ Universalists discount any teaching of an unforgivable sin

➢ Universalists believe that there are sources of religious truth outside the Judeo-Christian tradition.

➢ Universalists insist on a post-mortem chance at salvation.

➢ Universalists contend that the way to happiness is doing good

➢ Universalists believe that God will eventually redeem not only all humans but all of nature and Satan.

Universalists insist that God is perfect love and will eventually reach all humans through his omnipotent love. Universalists believe that all people will be restored to God. Universal Restoration springs from God's eternal grace and from Jesus who is the teacher who shows the Way (1 Tim 2:3-5), according to Ken R. Vincent (2005:5). Vincent concludes that "the Golden Thread of Universalism" begins with God's creation, continues through the Hebrew prophets, and culminates with Jesus' teachings. Jesus' ministry brings mankind to the Word and shows the Way so that all can recognize the Kingdom of God (Luke 17:20-21) (2005:72).

Eric Stetson declares:

> But Jesus Christ will "draw all people" to himself (John. 12:32) until "in Christ all will be made alive" (1 John. 4:8), so God would never abandon anyone to eternal punishment. God has a plan to rescue and transform even those who turned away from truth and goodness in this mortal life. Our heavenly Father will find every lost sheep and forgive every prodigal son! (2008).

Universalism claims to build its teachings on the concept of a loving and all-powerful God. An early advocate of Universalism, Thomas B. Thayer, placed Universalist teachings squarely on the doctrine of the love and power of God. He wrote:

> This is essentially the theology of Universalism the character and action which, following the sacred Scriptures, it ascribes to God as the Supreme Governor of the universe, and the Creator and Father of men. In him are united all possible perfections; and by the necessity of his nature, he is infinite in all his attributes, and unchangeable - the same yesterday, today, and forever. He is the source of all our blessing, the inexhaustible fountain of good to man in this world, and in all worlds, in time, and in eternity (1862:5).

Universalism affirms a perfect God. He is perfect love and is perfect in all his attributes. According to universalistic thinking, Calvinism limits his goodness. Simplified, it says: God can save all men, but he does not want to. Arminianism limits his power. It says: he wants to save all men, but cannot. Ron Bell sounds the view of Universalism when he states that God gets what he wants and declares, on the basis of 1 Tim 2:2, that God wants the salvation of all persons (2011:97-98). Bell asserts

> The writers of the scriptures consistently affirm that we're all part of the same family. What we have in common—regardless of our tribe, language, customs, beliefs, or religion—outweighs our differences. This is why God wants "all people to be saved." History is about the kind of love a parent has for a child, the kind of love that pursues, searches, creates, connects, and bonds. The kind of love that moves toward, embraces, and always works to be reconciled with, regardless of the cost (2011:99).

According to universalism, God's perfect love and power are not limited by human free will. When we limit God's goodness or power or wisdom, says Quillen Hamilton Shinn, we make him an imperfect God. If God is not perfect, there is no God. So this is atheism. Make what else of it you can (Shinn, nd. "Affirmations of Universalism").

A major conviction of almost all Universalists is the belief in a God of unlimited and perfect love who will call all people to himself. Less than universal salvation would, says Thomas

Only Jesus

Talbott, be contrary to the basic revelation of God's nature. Talbott writes that even evil depends for its existence upon the permission of God, who tolerates it temporarily because he can banish it from his creation forever. This well-known Universalist declares that it is obvious that even the annihilation of the wicked would represent a permanent defeat for a loving God and would leave a permanent stain on his creation. Nothing short, says Talbott, of every being reconciled to God and to each other in an inclusive community of love could possibly qualify as a decisive victory over evil (1999:201-202).

Universalism's vision of universal restoration rests firmly on the concept of a God of perfect love who will eventually reconcile all people to Himself. Richard Trudeau points out that John 14:16 rests at the center of Universalist thinking and has become the principal motto of the movement (2009:21). Bell seems to suggest that if God cannot and does not redeem all persons, God would have failed and is not so great and powerful as his followers have made him out to be (Bell 2011: 97-98; see Burk 2011:6).

Universalists contend that only this viewpoint does justice to the biblical teachings on the nature of God and His love. Obviously, a major plank in the Universalist platform relates to the salvation of *every* person. One Universalist publication states that God's eternal love will overcome even the hardest heart, that God's infinite patience will exhaust all rebellion, and that God's persistent grace will allow God to outlast the resistance of even the most rebellious. In other words, God's grace will never end (Gulley and Mulholland 2004:171).

Universalists project the teaching that Hell is temporary and corrective. They reject teachings of eternal separation or everlasting punishment that will be inflicted on humans. James A. Fowler in his critique of universalism points out that this approach denies the possibility of a final separation and segregation of mankind into eternally fixed categories of saved and lost (2004).

Most Universalists contend that eternal punishment is not a biblical teaching and that this teaching goes against all that God is and does. Rob Bell follows a long-established Universalistic view declaring that the biblical word "eternal" (*aion*) does not mean forever but rather indicates an *intensity of experience.* In Matt 25:46, Jesus does not speak of any eternal punishment but rather of a limited time of intense pruning that aids in restoring the sinner to eternal life (2011:91). Talbott adds that the word for punishment (*kolasis* had the meaning of suffering for remedial or corrective purposes (2003:47). He concludes that it is more reasonable to reject that Matt 25:46 teaches unending punishment and to affirm universal salvation on the basis of Rom 5:18 (Ibid).

About questions concerning the state of the wicked, Quillen Hamilton Shinn writes that those who are not cured of their evil in this world will be cured in the next. Shinn shows his aversion to teachings of eternal punishment as he says:

> What, then, is our answer to this question so perplexing to many anxious souls? This: Those who are not cured in this world and none are completely cured here, will be cured in the next. Old Orthodoxy says they will be sent to an eternal penitentiary. New Orthodoxy says they will establish themselves in endless rebellion against God, become eternal anarchists. The doctrine of annihilation, another phase of New Orthodoxy, says they will be blotted out of existence. Which answer can you best harmonize with the will and purpose and character of an infinitely good God? Universalism answers, *They will be cured.*

> The doctrine of endless brutality, politely called eternal punishment, must be utterly abhorrent to every thinking mind, revolting to every benevolent instinct. It is a hideous, ghastly, fiendish doctrine, heart-paralyzing, soul-stifling. It makes God infinitely worse than Nero, his malignancy transcending that of all the fiends of cruelty that ever lived. If true for only one soul, then that soul will receive more pain from the hands of God than the whole human family have received from all the monsters of brutality that have cursed our world; because there is no end to it. This doctrine is the great satanic blasphemy of the ages. Its ghastliness is monumental. It outpagans the blackest paganism! It ought to be a disgrace to preach the colossal infamy! It should cause the most brutal savage to blush with shame to listen to it! It has crushed more hearts, darkened more homes, caused more insanity and suffering and pain, it has made more infidels and atheists, than all other scourges that have ever desolated our

fair world? Oh, friends! I can't do it justice. I only wish I could make all men see its hideousness as I see it, and hate the infamous thing as I hate it! (nd. *Affirmations of Universalism*

http://www.auburn.edu/~allenkc/univart.html).

Eric Stetson echoes Shinn's denunciation of teachings on eternal punishment saying:

> There is no burning hell of torture where billions of souls who "sinned too much" or "chose the wrong religion" will suffer forever. Contrary to what most Christians today believe, such a horrible idea was not taught by Jesus and in not found anywhere in the original Hebrew Old Testament or Greek New Testament (2004,www.christianuniversalism.com).

In the eyes of universalists, Hell and eternal punishment simply do not exist nor will they exist. As seen earlier, John A. T. Robinson writes about the very nature of a God of love and that this love mitigates the truth of teachings of eternal punishment (1949: 155). Clark Pinnock, while not a universalist, expresses this belief of Universalism saying:

> . . . I consider the concept of hell as endless torment in body and mind an outrageous doctrine, a theological and moral enormity, a bad doctrine of the tradition which needs to be changed. How can Christians possibly project a deity of such cruelty and vindictiveness whose ways include inflicting everlasting torture upon his creature, however sinful they may have been? Surely a God who would do such a thing is more nearly like Satan than like God, at least by any moral standard, and by the gospel itself (1990: 246-47).

Obviously, Universalists teach that punishment for sin is redemptive or correctional not retributional. No concept of universalism suggests that sin does not result in negative experiences. As seen earlier, in 1899, the General Convention of Universalists formulated a brief statement of the five essential principles of the Universalist faith and the "Winchester Profession." The fourth of these statements of universalist belief proclaimed their conviction as to the certainty of just retribution for sin.

A Universalist statement affirms that God as moral governor of the universe will restore righteous and equitable rewards and punishments upon all mankind according to what they deserve. This statement also confirms the belief that all punishment will be remedial and therefore, limited.

Universalism does not question God's punishment for sin as just. Eric Stetson (2008) confirms that people do reap what they sow (Gal 6:7). Thomas Talbott simply declares that while eternal life, being rightly related to God is an end in itself, eternal punishment is a means to an end, and that end is remedial (2003:47). Talbott summarizes the Universalist position on the purpose of punishment insisting that Hell is remedial and the punishment wqas only intended as a means of correction. Hell is, contends Talbott, eternal only in the sense that its source lies in the eternal God himself and in the sense that it's corrective effects last forever. This state need not last any longer than is necessary to produce the end for which it exists in the first place (1999:91).

Universalism affirms punishment for sin but teaches that this punishment and the suffering will lead to cleansing and curing (Bell 2011:86 and 88). Talbott points out that the word punishment in *κολασιν αιωνιον* is specifically a term for and means nothing other than remedial punishment. The word was, he says, used for pruning of trees to make them grow better (1999: 91) and indicates that the punishment is inflicted in the interest of the sufferer rather than of the one who inflicts the suffering (2003:47).

Basically, the Christian Universalists believe that hell is temporary, a *reformative* punishment rather than vindictive and eternal. Ken Vincent reflects on the theology of Hosea Ballou who declared that God saves men in order to purify them. This is, says Ballou, what salvation is all about. Vincent reminds of Ballou's illustration that if a child falls into mud, the loving parent cleans the child and provides clean garments. You do not love the child, says Ballou, because you washed it but you washed it because you love it. Hell then, is for rehabilitation and does not last forever (Vincent 2005: 6).

Universalists question traditional theology, not about the existence of Hell, but about its purpose. Hell is not a place where God condemns people who failed to measure up to his standards and forces them to endure eternal and horrific tortures as a way to get revenge against them for failing to be or do what he commanded. Instead, say universalists, Hell is a way that God purifies humans of their imperfections, destroys the sinful nature within them, sets them straight, puts them through some necessary corrective experiences so that they may understand their failings, and can improve themselves so as to be ready to enter heaven (Ferré 1947:117; 1959:23). Packer, in his criticism of Universalism, shows that for Universalists, Hell is a house of corrections and place of grace and conversion. Saving evil persons from Hell is, according to Universalists, the ultimate triumph of God's love (2004:187).

Christian Universalists say their view of Hell is correct and the other view is a perverted fantasy about a sadistic god. Universalists are convinced that Hell is real for unrepentant sinners; it is not, in their view, a permanent state of being. Ken R. Vincent solves the problems relating to explicit biblical discussions of judgment and Hell. He points to what he calls "one of the least-known concepts in the biblical text," that is, he says, "Hell is not permanent." Hell is, says Vincent, for humankind's rehabilitation and that after a time of trial, all will be saved. Vincent bases these conclusions on Matthew 6:13 and 1 Timothy 4:10 (2005:24).

Universalists justify their thinking on Hell by referring to a list of scriptural materials. Packer writes that these verses to which Universalists point can be grouped in three linked classes of texts. One group, made up of six texts that Universalists think predicts the actual salvation of all people (John 12:32; Acts 3:21; Rom 5:18; 11:32; 1 Cor 15:22-28; Phil 2:9-11). A second group of biblical materials, they say, announce God's intention to save all (1 Tim 2:4; 2 Pet 3:9). A third group are seen to affirm that through Christ's redemptive death on the cross followed by his resurrection and dominion, God must and will eventually save all (2 Cor 5:19; Gal 1:20; Titus 2:11; Heb 2:9; 1 John 2:2). Packer points out that Universalists contend that the use of the terms "all" and "world" in these passages support their viewpoint on eternal punishment (see Packer 2004:187).

Universalists insist that early Christianity held to the doctrine of universal restoration and did not subscribe to the teachings of eternal punishment. As seen earlier, John Wesley Hanson traces the current teachings of endless torment or eternal punishment to errors of the Western Church and teachers such as Augustine. Universalism was, says Hanson, the prevailing doctrine of the Christian church during its first five hundred years (1899:21-26). In a more contemporary work, Gregory McDonald agrees saying that some Universalists have argued that universal restoration was the prevailing view of the church in its first five hundred years. The view that hell is an everlasting punishment is, they maintain, a theology that arose as pagan thinking infected the church. So, contend these Universalists, the purer, more original Christianity is Universalist, and those who affirm everlasting hell are the true heretics. They believe that the teaching that all will be saved is the gospel itself—the true heart of Christian faith (2011:3).

In his early theological treatise, Hanson speaks warmly of Hosea Ballou's work that also maintained belief in the doctrine of universal salvation in the early church (Ibid. 1-2). Hanson concludes, "Thus the creedal declarations of the Christian church for almost four hundred years were entirely void of the lurid doctrine with which they afterwards blazed for more than a thousand years" (1899:15).

Many Universalists point to the early Christian theologian, Origen, as a teacher of *apokatastasis* or universalism. These Universalists point to Origen's statements that promised the total and ultimate restitution of all things and all persons. Origen, say Universalists, taught that God would win a complete victory and all things would become as in the first condition. Nothing and no one would be life unredeemed (*Contra Celsus*; see Mohler 2004:17). Further, Universalists quote Origen as holding that Hell would be purifying, corrective, and temporary rather than punitive.

Universalists see their doctrines as being the original teachings that were changed by such leaders as Augustine. In this line of thinking, Universalism stands outside the actual teachings of Christian history. In his warning about the danger of leaving the teachings on Hell out of Christian theology, Albert Mohler laments the loss of the teaching (2004:16). Christopher Morgan and Robert Peterson show that a biblical view of Hell is intimately tied to other scriptural teachings such as the enormity of sin, the intense love of the atonement, the unquestioned holiness of God, the enormous cost of the death of Christ, and the imperative of the

Only Jesus

preaching of the full gospel (2004:240).

Universalists insist that they hold a high view of the value of humans. Universalism affirms belief in human nature and the worth of man. The divine Fatherhood indicates that man fashioned in God's image is of infinite value. Because humans are created in the image of God, no person will be destroyed or lost. God cannot destroy a thing that is indestructible. Wrapped up in this divine embryo are capacities and powers that fit man for endless growth and progress assurance of endless growth.

In this sense, say universalists, the spiritual perfection reached by God's children will be relative. Man is not made, he is making. Those who have made greatest progress are still in the Father's primary school. There will be higher departments, one grade leading to another, on and up forever. The school of God will never let out. Humans should exult because God has eternity to train his children. Universalists claim to hold the supreme possibilities in humankind.

Universalism affirms belief in inherent immortality. Without this divine inheritance what can man do to become immortal? No more than a tree. The trouble is that Christian people have failed to make a distinction between immortal life and eternal life. It was a part of Christ's mission to *reveal* immortality but no part of his mission to create it. Immortal life has reference to duration; eternal life to quality. Jesus said, *"This is life eternal, to know thee the only true God and Jesus Christ whom thou hast sent"* (John 17:3). Christians can, says Vincent, be confident in the theology of Universal restoration (2005:7).

Universalism, clearly, stands for the worth of man. The child, however frail, is of infinite value in his Father's sight. God has not given to even one of his children the power to sin himself out of existence or place himself beyond the reach of love. No human being has power to defeat the purpose of the Infinite One. Every soul is worth saving, and according to the teachings of universalism *will be saved.* Universalists believe no human is so unimportant that God will give up on him or her. God will save all humans because they are created in his image (Talbott 2003:3-14).

Universalists discount any teaching of an unforgiv-

able sin. Thomas Talbott in relation to the unforgivable sin writes that the better question concerning this matter is, "Just what does it mean to say the God will never forgive or pardon a given sin?" Does it mean, he asks, that God no longer loves or seeks to reconcile the person who commits that particular sin?

An unforgivable sin, says Talbott, is not an uncorrectable sin at all. It is simply a sin that God cannot deal with adequately in the absence of appropriate punishment. Even the punishment for sin mentioned in Hebrews 10:26, 27, continues Talbott, is actually an expression of mercy. It will refine and correct the sin and eventuate in the sinner returning to God (1999:103-104).

Universalists believe that there are sources of religious truth outside the Judeo-Christian tradition. The Universalists belief that God's love is universal impels them to hold that God loves everybody. Ken R. Vincent declares that the basic teachings of Universalism require a different view of world religions. If, he says, all are saved then other paths to God must have some validity (2005:6).

That truth is found in other traditions is plain from Universalist teachings that God loves those in areas far from the lands of Moses or Jesus. For this reason, God sent messengers or teachers to other lands—for example, Siddhartha Gautama to India and Lao-Tzu to China. The religions that such teachers founded (Buddhism, Taoism) also are sources of religious truth as is Christianity (Trudeau 2009:20).

In regard to this teaching, some Universalists seem to be fully in the camp of the group known as inclusivists. Ron Bell, while declaring he is not a Universalist, moves into what is definitely inclusivist thinking saying:

> There is inclusivity. The kind that is open to all religions, the kind that trusts that good people will get in, that there is only one mountain, but it has many paths. This inclusivity assumes that as long as your heart is fine or your actions measure up, you'll be okay (2011:155).

Differences do remain between Universalists and Inclusivists. The similarities, however, indicate the possibility that universalism should be included among the wider-hope theories.

Universalists contend that people will have a post-mortem chance at salvation. Samuel Cox speaks passionately about the plight of the many that have had little or no opportunity to respond to the message of Salvation in Christ. He states his difficulty in denying these people any chance at life with God. Cox's solution is a post-mortem opportunity. He writes:

> What *shall* we say then? For myself I can only say that I see no way out of the difficulty, no single loop-hole of escape, so long as we assume what the Bible does not teach, that there is no probation beyond the grave, that no moral change is possible in that world towards which all the children of time are traveling. I, at least, am so sure that the Father of all men will do the most and best which can be done for every man's salvation as to entertain no doubt that long ere this the men of Sodom and of Tyre and Sidon have heard the words of Christ and seen his mighty works - seen and heard Him, perchance, when He stood and shone among the spirits in the Hadean prison, and preached the gospel to them that were dead, in order that, while still judged according to men in the flesh, they might live according to God in the spirit (1 Peter 3:19-20; 4:6) (1899:6-7).

Speaking of the Lord's words about future punishment, Cox declares that these words must mean at least that in the future, as in the present, there will be diversities of moral condition, and a discipline nicely adapted to those diversities? Cox writes:

> May they not mean that those who have sinned against a little light will, after having been chastened for their sins with a "few stripes," receive more light, and be free to walk in it if they will? We are often chastened in this world that we may not be condemned with the World, often judged and condemned and punished that we may be aroused to repentance and saved unto life everlasting. Why, then, should we always take the chastenings of the world to come to mean judgments, and the judgments to mean condemnations, and the condemnations to mean nothing short of a final and irreversible doom? On the contrary,

we ought rather to hope that while during the brief hours of time our lives describe but "broken arcs," in eternity, and through whatever chastening and discipline may be requisite for us, they will reach "the perfect round" (Cox 1899).

Universalists uphold the teaching of opportunities for repentance after human death. Most Universalists maintain exactly this conviction. Universalists share this belief with many in the other camps of Wider-hope theories. Proponents of Post-mortem Evangelism (sometimes designed P. M. E.) try to uphold universal accessibility but also the understanding that salvation can only come by special revelation and an explicit confession of faith in Jesus Christ. Daniel Strange in criticizing this view shows that driven by human logic, advocates of P. M. E. conceive of a meeting with the Risen Christ after death—a meeting at which these will be able to accept or reject him (Strange 2002:322).

Some Wider-hope followers see the possibility of either acceptance or rejection in this meeting. John Sanders, while agreeing with Talbott that Post-mortem opportunity for repentance is a reality, shows his disagreement with the idea that every person will repent. He declares that Universalists believe that every single person will come to the proper decision in this face-to-face, post-mortem encounter with the risen Lord. That every person will repent is questioned by Sanders (Sanders 2003: 170-71). Philip Gulley and James Mulholland proclaim the "Persistence of God" and remain absolutely convinced that ". . . God will save *every person*" (2004:161).

These writers continue to hold the teaching of "Grace beyond the Grave" (Ibid. 168). Using the parables of the lost coin, the absent landowner, and the loving father (the prodigal son) Gulley and Mulholland contend that God's love and seeking will persist even after death (Ibid, 161-70).

Universalists contend that the way to happiness is doing good. The loving God of Universalism desires that people be happy. Hosea Ballou, a noted Universalist, coined the term "happify" in saying that God wants to "happify" people now. "In Universalism, the reward for doing good is not salvation in a possible next life but what happiness in this one" (Trudeau 2009:20).

Only Jesus

Universalism contends that good works among human-kind is a major factor in true Christianity. Shinn writes:

Every deed of mercy that lessens pain; every charity that assuages sorrow and distress; every church that throws its arms of love around the wayfaring man; every institution of learning that kindles thoughts of a higher world; every new discovery disclosing larger visions of truth; every fresh avenue of commerce opening wider channels for the diffusion of God's love; every object lesson in this great outer world teaching Gods bounty and care; every flower preaching its sermon of beauty by the wayside; every star that looks down from the upper deeps, kindling the sense of mystery and wonder in the human breast; every cloud sleeping in the azure heights, serene with suggestions of peace; every setting sun painting the sky, and turning to gold the retreating clouds; every breeze that wafts the incense of healing and of hope; every ray of light that breaks the films of sin, to let love into the hardened heart; every drop of water that revives the drooping plant; every fountain breaking from the mountain side; every brooklet singing its glad song; every sparkling lake catching in its dimples the colors of the sky; every river flowing down and mingling in the sea; every ocean that sends up its mists to fill the clouds-- all teaching the goodness and bounty of God; every experience that deepens human life; every sorrow that sweetens the spirit; every pain that chisels and refines; every new-born hope lifting the tendrils of a shattered faith; every anguish that plows the soul, cleansing the grosser man; every defeat that breaks the defiant will; every throb of sympathy pulsing from heart to heart; every pang of remorse that makes sin ghastly, and turns its victim into the path of life; every blaze of light revealing to groping souls the awful darkness that domes the sinners sky; every strain of music reviving sweet memories of the past; every sunny face that lights up the home of man; every voice of childhood prattling the song of trust; every angel God sends into this world to nurse back to life and health the lost of earth, and lead them up the celestial highway, the King's highway, from glory unto glory, and at last into the resplendent light of the perfect day,-- all, all these are agents, messengers, instruments, to fulfill the sublime prophecy of our Universalist faith ,--final triumph, glorious victory! -- instruments breathed upon from higher worlds, and weaving their countless strains for the grand, triumphant, joyous, matchless symphony of God! (nd. http://www.auburn.edu/~allenkc/univart.html).

Universalists believe that God will eventually redeem not only all humans but all of nature and Satan. Universalist teachers often point with agreement to the theologian Origen who declared that God will in the end redeem even Satan, the Prince of Darkness (Patrides 1967: 469). Even though Origen later rejected this teaching it was restated by Jerome who wrote that the Apostate Angel would return to his first estate (Talbott 1999:15). The teachings of Universalists leaders insist that redemption will be complete and all will be brought finally to salvation (Ibid. 67-69).

But what of such massive sinners as Adolf Hitler and Adolf Eichmann? Universalists answer that such persons must recognize the enormity of their sins. They must reclaim enough of their humanity to admit their wrong and appreciate why they were wrong. When these sinful persons begin to understand their sinfulness and the true nature of their evil deeds, redemption can begin. As seen earlier, Universalists believe that a just order will only be restored when Hitlers and Eichmanns come to love their victims so tenderly that they would gladly suffer on their behalf as they have already suffered due to the evil deeds of these corrupt people (Talbott 1999:167, 197). Ferré with incredible confidence writes:

> Without the ultimate salvation of all creatures, men and, we think, animals [and birds? and insects? and fish? and reptiles? Presumably so] in God's time and way, it is easy to see that there can be no full solution of the problem of evil (1946; 117).

As God's moral nature and love is simple, so is God's justice. Both require the absolute destruction of sin and that sinners repent of the wrong they have done to God and others. Such a final restitution of all things alone would qualify as the triumph of justice (Talbott 1999:167). The logic of universalism demands this final and total victory of God over all evil.

Universalists, thus, envision the salvation of all. The monstrous sinners of human history and the Prince of Darkness himself will return to God, their maker. For Universalists, *universal Restoration* is the result of God's eternal grace and Jesus is the teacher who shows us the way (Vincent 2005:5).

Evaluation of Universalism

How should Evangelical Christians look at Universalism and its teachings? Certainly, anyone who considers the tragedy of eternal separation from God must be attracted by the teachings of Universalism. It erases the desperate questions of loved ones who have died without expressing faith in Christ and the multitudes who had little or no chance of responding to him. Believers who are aware of the infinite loss of eternal separation would gladly welcome such a wider-hope alternative if it were true.

Evangelicals are equally dedicated to believing what the Bible reveals *and no more than that*. However comforting or tempting an alternative to biblical teaching might seem, Evangelicals must rest solely on God's revelation. The teaching of the infallible Word of God remains the bedrock for Evangelical belief even when that teaching drives him/her to places that are difficult and uncomfortable. We turn to an evaluation of Universalism from an Evangelical standpoint.[*]

Evangelicals applaud the concern for the unreached expressed in Universalist thinking and also the commitment of Universalists to Christian living and service. Rob Bell, from his insistence that he is not Universalistic, sounds the often heard refrain of heartbreak at the thought of such a large segment of humanity being eternally separated from God and goodness (2011:1-10). Evangelicals join in such remorse.

Evangelicals join many Universalists in questions about the eternal status of unusually gifted persons, such as Gandhi. Philip Gulley and James Mulholland sketch their journey that led to an inability to believe Gandhi and such people were among the damned (2004:161-65). The difficulty in dealing with the eternal destiny of real people is a problem

---

[*]Readers will easily understand that many of the evaluations in regard to Universalism will also apply to other wider-hope theories.

for Universalists and Evangelicals recognize the desire for people and God's will for people. These feelings of concern are commendable.

Evangelicals also join in the Universalists conviction that belief in Christ should make a difference in the lives of the believers. Believers in Christ participate in his nature and by virtue of their new life in Christ move into the world to make differences in human situations. Evangelicals agree with the Universalists' desire to work toward a better world.

Evangelicals stand on the teaching that a vast difference exists between those who follow Jehovah, God, and those who adhere to other religions. The Apostle Paul indicated his intense desire for the conversion and salvation of his fellow Jewish people. They were religious but were attempting by Law keeping to establish their own right-standing with God and were therefore separated from His salvation. These verses strongly indicate that religion is insufficient to make one right with God. The Apostle wrote:

> Brothers and sisters, my heart's desire and prayer to God for the Israelites is that they may be saved. [2] For I can testify about them that they are zealous for God, but their zeal is not based on knowledge. [3] Since they did not know the righteousness of God and sought to establish their own, they did not submit to God's righteousness. [4] Christ is the culmination of the law so that there may be righteousness for everyone who believes (Rom 10:14 NIV).

Evangelicals should not put down other religions and the adherents of them. God's servants should assume no stance of superiority or greater knowledge. Harold Netland has eloquently taught us that those seeking to share the Good News with followers of other religions must, however, clothe ourselves with the unshakable conviction of the full truth and authority of God's Word and the indispensability of the gospel of Jesus Christ as "the power of God for the salvation of everyone who believes, first for the Jew, then for the Gentile" (Rom 1:16).

This sharing will avoid any hint of religious arrogance or imperialism. The effort is one of sharing in the humble recognition that each of us is but a sinner saved by God's grace and the assurance that what the Lord has done for us he will do for others—including those now committed to other Faiths (see Netland 1995: 262-63)

Evangelicals, while affirming the biblical teachings of God's expansive love and intense desire for people, recognize that the Love of God does not cancel his justice. Some Universalists seem to teach that God's love will override or cancel his justice, holiness, and wrath at sin. They seem to contend that God, the Almighty, will of necessity remain faithful to his entire nature.

Evangelicals, on the other hand, believe that God has revealed that his justice allows humans the free will to choose the way of destruction and separation. Alister E. McGrath speaks of the Christian (evangelical) view of the love of God that is a vulnerable love offered to us through Christ. This theologian points out that Universalism denies humanity the right to say no to God, in essence to be predestined to be saved. McGrath understands this problem to be analogous to the same problems associated with the approach of John Calvin in relation to divine sovereignty and human responsibility (1995:177).

Evangelical theology holds in concert the teachings of God's love and his punishment of sin. God's love and justice cannot be divided or separated. "God always acts in ways that perfectly and harmoniously express his love, holiness, wrath against sin, and injustice" (Ott, Strauss, and Tennent 2010: 329). John Piper correctly observes that God's love does not imply that God relates to persons only in terms of love (1983:11).

David Wells sounds the same note saying that an error in modernism is the concept that God's love exhausts the biblical imagery of the deity (1994:135). God's love must be understood in concert with his other attributes and one of these "other" attributes is judgment. John Frame expresses the danger of failing to view all of the attributes of God. He speaks of the attributes of God as being perspectival, that is each of them describing everything that God is from a different perspective (2001:53-54).

God's love also must be understood in light of the seriousness of sin and rebellion against this love. Sin is rebellion by finite persons against the Creator who is infinite. Once an interpreter comprehends the true tragedy and wickedness of sin, the concept of its punishment becomes understandable. God's love can only become clear from the vantage of a realization of the seriousness of sin. Human wisdom tends to see the consequences of sin as too great and serious. Viewed from the view of the depth of sinfulness, however, punishment can be understood clearly as appropriate. J. I. Packer reacts to this line of thinking concluding:

> . . . those who seek to explain away hell in order to safeguard God's moral praiseworthiness fail to see that New Testament authors saw hell not as creating a moral problem but as resolving one—namely, the problem of rebellious evil and human cruelty being allowed to run loose in God's world (2004:67).

John Piper offers an important insight. He teaches that sin is idolatry, the placing of human values in the place of honor and respect to God. Hell is, Piper says, ". . . designed to make clear the infinite value of God's glory and the moral horror of idolatry" (2010: Kindle Edition location 514). He concludes:

> There is an idolatry in all our sins—a valuing of something more than God. Hell is God's declaration to the universe that what every sin demeans is of infinite worth (Ibid).
>
> Evangelicals think that wider-hope theories in general exalt the love of God and overlook his justice and judgment. A balance in our thinking about God requires that all biblical teachings about his attributes be considered and kept in balance. The certain teachings of the love of God must never eliminate the teachings of his wrath against sin and his judgment against evil.

Evangelicals find promise of salvation only after a conscious decision to unite with Christ during a person's lifetime. They find no Scriptural support for either postmortem salvation possibility or conditional immorality (annilationism). The view of most Exclusivists is summed up in the words of I. Howard Marshall who declares that the teaching of the New Testament authors is that there will be a final judgment and that the outcome of this judgment will be justification for some and condemnation for others. No indication that these outcomes are anything other than final exists in biblical teachings, says Marshall (2003:56).

In his discussion of those who have never heard, Gabriel Fackre suggests that the answer to this recurring question lies in his concept of "divine perseverance." In defining divine perseverance, Fackre contends that theologians need a better expression of the meaning of divine perseverance. This idea, says Fackre, has previously been restricted to the perseverance of the saints and their power never to backslide. Fackre intends to use the term to speak of the perseverance of God and teach that God will never give up on spreading his message. He concludes saying:

> In this world God will give us the power to spread the gospel far and wide. But the Word will also be declared to those we can't reach, even if it takes an eternity. I am convinced the poet Francis Thompson had it right—Christ is the "Hound of Heaven" pursuing us to the end (1995:73).

In his response to this teaching, Ronald Nash, warns against taking Fackre's assumptions as though they were well-established conclusions. After carefully showing the limitations of Fackre's interpretations of Scripture, Nash concludes, "Fackre's theory of salvation after death lacks biblical support" (1995). Most evangelicals would side with Nash's views concerning this discussion.

Evangelicals also do not accept Thomas Talbott's interpretation that Rom 5:12-21 establishes universal reconciliation. In the face of I. Howard Marshall's contention that no biblical evidence exists for postmortem salvation, Talbott writes:

> The absence of a clear statement in the Bible affirming post-mortem repentance would be no evidence at all against such repentance. But within the context of a shared assumption concerning the reality of post-mortem judgement [sic], the presence of a clear statement that Christ's one 'act of righteousness lead to justification and life for all' humans could be conclusive evidence that such judgement will terminate in post-mortem repentance (2003:256).

John Piper strenuously disagrees with the interpretation that Romans 5:18 or any of the other "all" statements in Paul's writings indicate that every person will be saved. He points out that verse 17 indicates that eternal life is for *all who receive the gift of righteousness*. Some obviously do not receive it, says Piper. He refers to Rom 2:5, 3:28, and 5:1 to show that this "all" statement is not automatic but rather by faith. Piper's conclusion is "A universalistic reading of Paul's 'all' statements renders Paul's intense grief (Romans 9:3)—to the point of wishing he could perish, if possible on their behalf—unintelligible" (2002:108 n).

Evangelicals also do not accept Talbott's beautiful but mistaken view of who will enter Heaven. Talbott writes:

> . . . even the kings of the earth, those most vile of all men who had stood with the beasts and the false prophet (Rev 19:19), are seen entering the New Jeru-salem. So from whence do they come? Outside are the . . . fornicators and murders and idolaters, and every-one who loves and practices falsehood (22:15'; outside is the lake of fire, the only reality left apart from the New Jerusalem itself. 'But nothing unclean will enter' (21:27), we are also told. So something must happen in the lake of fire to enable the kings of the earth and others to enter the City from the only possible position outside its gates, and that something is surely repent-ance and a thorough cleansing of a kind that implies a proper relationship with Jesus Christ (2003;256-57).

Evangelicals accept the interpretations of writers such as I. Howard Marshall and Christopher W. Morgan (2003; 2004) both of whom clearly show the misunderstandings in univer-salistic teachings. Marshall states that Paul's teaching in Rom 5:12-21 describes the salvation of persons who believe and accept God's salvation offer. We have no evidence for a post-mortem opportunity to believe in this passage, or in the rest of the New Testament, says Marshall. We can, there-fore, not assume that all individuals will be saved or have the after death opportunity (2003: 65). Marshall concludes saying, "There is nowhere any suggestion that the final judgment still leaves the door open for repentance" (2003:72). He concludes:

Only Jesus

The New Testament does not teach nor imply universal salvation. It teaches the reality of a final judgement on the impenitent and sadly it states that some will be lost. That is why there is such an urgency to proclaim the gospel to all the world (2003:74).

Evangelicals accept the biblical teaching of the permanency of Hell and punishment. Evangelicals believe the term "everlasting" means just that and do not accept the wider-hope attempts to change the term "everlasting" (*aion*) into something more limited. With no joy at the fact, exclusivists accept the biblical teaching that separation from God (Hell) involves both eternal and conscious punishment for rebellion (see Ott, Strauss, and Tennent 2010: 326-28).

Exclusivists accept the teaching of the Old Testament that many who are asleep in the dust will awake on the fateful day. Some will awake to everlasting life but others to disgrace and everlasting contempt. Daniel Block points out that in this passage "life" means the recovery of all that for which humankind was created, free and open fellowship with God and all the privileges associated with that relationship. The revulsion and loathing ascribed to the wicked is "eternal" like the "life" of the righteous. The word 'oläm, as Block teaches, means not the end of an epoch but rather time without end (2004:64). The imagery of this passage leaves no room for changing the meaning of "everlasting."

Teachings in Isaiah 66:24 along with Matt 18:8-9 and Mark 9:42-49 imply that the suffering noted goes on forever and without end (see Ott, Strauss, Tennent 2010:326). Christopher Morgan points out that Jesus directly relates that Hell is a place of "eternal fire" and "fire that does not go out" (2004:138). Particularists accept the teaching that Hell is real (not metaphorical), it is a place of separation and deprivation, of pain and punishment, of darkness and destruction, and of disintegration and perishing (Ferguson 2004:226-27).

Exclusivists interpret the New Testament as teaching clearly that separation is forever. The Lord's words in Matt 25:46 relate the same term, "eternal" to the punishment of the evil ones and the life of the righteous. The same teaching rests in John 3:16; 5:24, and 5:29. The conclusion of the exclusivist is that the same meaning should be given to eternal separation as to eternal life. This conclusion leads to the conviction that separation and life are both unending (see Yarbrough 2004:75-78).

The Apostle Paul points to Hell as eternal separation but also as destruction (2 Thess 1:8-10). While many seek to understand "destruction" in this verse to mean extinction (Edwards and Stott 1988:316) the actual meaning is that which has lost the essence of its nature or function (Moo 2004:105). The teachings of Paul do not support any sort of universalism or conditionalism (*anniliahionism*).

The Apostle John in *The Revelation* points out both the eternal nature of Hell and the conscious state of those who confine themselves to that place (Rev. 14:9-12; 20:10). Exclusivists see no "chiasm" in Rev 14:11. Revelation presents the terror of Hell as eternal and unending. Gregory K. Beale teaches that one without a prior theological agenda to defend a particular view of divine love and justice would hardly deny that the judgment of all unbelieving humans would be different from the devil and his angels. Beale is convinced that the punishments from the devil and unbelieving persons will the same, especially the punishments seen in Revelation 14 and 20 (2004:134).

Christopher W. Morgan clearly sets forth the Exclusivist view on eternal punishment that the biblical teaching of God's ultimate victory over Satan and evil is compatible with the endless punishment of the wicked. Morgan contends this is the most natural interpretation of Rev 20:10. Morgan's conclusion is that Hell will continue forever and God's victory will be complete (2004:217-18).

The idea that Hell is temporary and a place of purifying the sinners or giving them a second chance is, in the thinking of exclusivists, unbiblical in the sense that it is not found in the Bible. These basic teachings of Universalists (and other wider-hope teachers) does not equate with the Exclusivist's interpretation or understanding of Scripture. This point concerning the eternal nature of Hell and its punishments on the unsaved divides Exclusivists from the wider-hope teachings. The Exclusivists conclusion is "The consistent witness of scripture seems to be that some people will suffer eternal, conscious punishment for their rebellious rejection of God" (Ott, Strauss, Tennent 2010:328).

Only Jesus

Evangelicals affirm that any who suffer in eternal torment do so at their own choice. Christopher W. Morgan states that "The punishment is deserved and therefore *just*" (2004:143). Jesus indicated in the "sheep and goats" passage that good reason existed for the separation of the people into those who would enter their inheritance, the Kingdom prepared for them and those consigned to depart into the eternal fire, prepared for the devil and his angels (Matt 25:31-46). Passages such as 2 Thess 1:5-12 and 2 Pet 2:17-22 indicate that the desperate situation of the wicked rests on their own actions.

Evangelicals hear and understand the words of Universalists about a good God being too pure to allow any evil to remain. Talbott has written:

> So herein lies the Christian universalists's understanding of God's ultimate victory, which is also a key to proper understanding of divine judgement. God is too pure (read 'too loving') to allow evil of any kind to survive forever in his creation. He will not, therefore, merely quarantine evil in hell, but will instead destroy it altogether even as he regenerates the evil ones themselves (2003:26).

Evangelicals would with gratitude accept this teaching. No one takes joy at thinking of any in eternal separation from God and good. Evangelicals do not, however, make God the villain in any future punishment. Neither do Exclusivists have any idea that an eternal separation and punishment would indicate lack of power or weakness in God.

People place themselves in this condition. The responsibility is on the evil ones. The reason for eternal punishment is not due to God's uncaring spirit or limited ability to act. People go out to an eternal separation because they reject the loving, continuing, and costly invitation of God in Christ. Carl Henry writes:

> God's fairness is demonstrated because he condemns sinners not in the absence of light but because of their rebellious response. His mercy is demonstrated because he provides fallen humans with a privileged call to redemption not extended to fallen angels. He continues to extend that call worldwide even while some rebel humans spurn it as unloving and unjust and pre-

fer to die in their sins. All are judged by what they do with the light they have, and none is without light (1991:255).

Particularists uphold the biblical teaching relating to the freedom of humankind to decide—even to decide to turn away from God's offer of salvation. McGrath shows the problem of such a statement saying that the idea that all will be saved involves the teaching that all will consent to be saved. The final situation is, says McGrath, one in which God imposes his salvation on humans. McGrath correctly points out that the optimistic affirmation that "all will be saved" easily turns to the pronouncement "all must be saved whether they like it or not" (1995:177).

The Exclusivist position is summed up:

> God's love, justice, holiness, and wrath against sin converge on the cross of Christ, the greatest expression of his love (John 3:16; Rom 5:8; 1 John 4:10). In Christ, God has provided a way that is sufficient and available for all people to be reconciled to him. All who end up eternally separated from God will have already chosen to reject God and separate themselves from him in this life. Hell will be the extension of that decision throughout eternity (Ott, Strauss, and Tennent 2010: 329).

Evangelicals agree to the total necessity of world evangelism and world service in every generation. The great Commission remains as valid and essential marching orders for Evangelicals. Rejection of all wider-hope theories, including Universalism, requires a missionary response. If all are separated from God by sin and evil, and if the one cure for this condition is personal faith in Jesus Christ, and if the Message of Christ is needed to turn humans to the faith that saves, then, Christians must respond, proclaim this truth to all, and lead them into to grace of God's salvation (see Ott, Strauss, Tennent 2010:337).

Evangelicals also will hear when many point out the relative failure of Christians to reach the point of social justice taught in biblical sources. This charge is partially true. Christians who disbelieve in the teachings of wider-hope theories must undertake not only world evangelism but also world service. Believers in Jesus Christ cannot stand idle in the face of mass lostness, widespread physical neediness, or crippling social injustice.

Conclusion

E. A. Blum declares that the major apologetic against universalism must be that it is unbiblical and unchristian. Its major concept, sovereign love, comes from humanistic orientations rather than biblical exegesis. The concepts of universalism create more problems than they solve. For those involved in evangelism, the consequences of rejecting universalism should it be true are far less than the terrible tragedy of accepting it if it is incorrect. Blum's conclusion strikingly expresses this evaluation of universalism:

> Finally, if the universalist position be correct, no lasting damage would have been done. But if the issues are as Jesus and the Christian church have proclaimed, the momentous nature of the decision concerning Christ's sacrifice is apparent. The choice is then—life or death (Blum 1979:61).

Neither Universalism nor Conditionalism (annihilationsim) provides a reason for Particularists to move into the teachings of any wider-hope theory.

Those who hold the Particularistic viewpoint on salvation should, however, be alert to the criticism that those in our camp have at times at least given the impression that they have overlooked the clear teachings of the Bible as to God's intention that his people engage in social action to change the world and minister to the needy. Such teaching is obviously a central concept in biblical theology and must ever be a major part of evangelical life and ministry. Proper concern for the poor and needy that stems from the will of the Father never detracts from true evangelism.

CHAPTER 3

THE PLURALISTIC
APPROACH

Another wider-hope theory, Pluralism, answers the question, "Is Jesus the only Savior?" with a definite, "no!" Paul Knitter, as seen earlier, calls this approach the Mutuality Position. Pluralists maintain that no one religion is unique or superior in providing salvation, which Pluralists define as access to the Divine Reality (Knitter 2005: vii).

The Pluralist viewpoint believes that the major world religions provide independent saving access to the divine Reality (see Gilkey 1987:37-50). Gary P. Stewart, in his criticism of Pluralism, remarks that "pluralism understands that there are many different animals in the zoo who live in many different cages" (2000: 370). As will be seen, many writers who are not always placed in the category of Pluralists write in ways that reflect pluralist teachings.

John Hick, for example, contends that the world religions provide "soteriological spaces" or ways by which people find salvation, liberation, ultimate, or fulfillment (1989:240). Raimundo Panikkar declares that in the present time neither exclusivism nor inclusivism represents the proper attitude. Only pluralism, he contends, is the correct response to the present situation (1987:103).

Bruce J. Nicholls criticizes Pluralism describing it as the "mark of our age." He declares that Pluralism claims that it is axiomatic that no one religion can claim uniqueness and finality and that no religious founder can claim to be the only savior of the world (1994:9). Stanley Samartha proves Nichol's point insisting that it is preposterous for any religion to claim to be the only answer to the global problems confronting humankind (1988:315).

The strong pluralist tendency seen among many Christian authors is also expressed in leaders of other religions. Bibhuti S. Yadav, for example, quotes Gandhi as saying that he believed the *Gita* and indeed regarded all the great faiths of the world as equally true with his own (1990:235). Yadav continues by stating that humanist philosophies declare that one inflicts injury upon his own religion by devaluating the religions of others. He then refers to Radharkrishnan as teaching that the Absolute is active in all religions. He concludes:

> To claim "special revelation" for a religion is anthropomorphic; it is an argument to kill the Absolute and to enthrone oneself as Absolute. Radhakrishan further argued that the Absolute is larger than it revelations, that no revelation is an absolutely true as the Absolute, and that all revelations are equally true but relative in relation to the Absolute (1990:236).

The pluralist concept rejects all three of the basic nonnegotiables that exclusivists hold imperative (Ott, Strauss, Tennent 2010:299). Pluralism basically projects relativism upon the world's thinking. Ernest Hocking in 1931 declared Christianity to be *only one* of the living religions that seeks to help humanity with the quest of the eternal. Other religions share in this quest. All religions, including Christianity, aid humans in finding the righteous way and life and in transforming society through an evolutionary process. It is not the Christian duty to attack the non-Christian religions but rather to help them speak for themselves. The purpose of mission, according to Hocking, is not conversion but to join the other religions in the efforts against secularism (1932:325-27).

Arnold Toynbee reflects the same tendencies so often seen in Pluralistic teachings. He declares that Christianity should purge itself of any idea it is the exclusive religion. Christianity, says Toynbee, should join Buddhism and guide humanity out of the problems caused by human selfishness (1957). John Hick obviously follows this line of thinking saying that Christianity in a pluralistic context is seen as "one of the great world faiths, one of the streams of religious life through which human beings can be savingly related to that ultimate Reality Christians know as the heavenly Father" (1988:22).

Pluralism obviously conflicts with the entire spirit of Only Jesus. James E. Chancellor, in his critique of Pluralism, declares that Pluralism is obviously correct in his observation that "the ideology of religious pluralism must tolerate all views of the Absolute, except those that lay claim to absolute truth" (1994:536).

Basic Teachings of Pluralism

John Hick, along with other Pluralists such as Ernst Troeltsch William Hocking, Paul Knitter, William Cantwell Smith, Langdon Gilkey, and Tom F. Driver, believes that the world religions are as true and as effective in reaching liberation, freedom, or salvation as Christianity. These writers affirm that all religions are valid and deny that Christianity is the one true religion, the highest religion, or the fulfillment of other religions. Pluralists declare that no religion may truthfully claim supremacy and they call on Christianity to surrender its claims to exclusivity (Hick and Knitter 1987:33; Sanders 1992: 115; Knitter 2005: vii-xi).

Paul Knitter thinks it important that Christians and Christianity move beyond their ideas of Christian superiority. He calls for Christians to reach an understanding of the uniqueness or distinctiveness of Christ and Christianity so that they would no longer need to insist that they have the only, the final, or the superior path to God and absolute Truth. Christianity should, he says, remain important and distinctive, but so would other religions (2005 vii).

No one path to salvation exists according to John Hick. He teaches that *many ways exist*—all taking place differently within the contexts of the religious traditions (Hick and Knitter 1987:16-36; Hick 1985: 34; 1987:16-36). In fact, Hick summarizes his position with a verse from the Hindu Holy Book, The *Bhagavad Gita*, *"Howsoever man may approach me, even so do I accept them; for, on all sides, whatever path they may choose is mine"* (1980a:71-79; 1980b:125-26).

Pluralists hold that, while there is only one Ultimate Reality, this Reality is properly, though only partially, understood in different ways (See Runzo 1988:51). Pluralism contends that inclusivism does not go far enough in affirming salvation in all religions (Driver 1987: 203-205). For convicted Pluralists, salvation is found not in discovering Christ *in* other religions but *within* these religions themselves.

Paul Knitter has taken the idea of living within the religions to a new level. As seen earlier, he claims to have become a Buddhist while remaining a Christian. Knitter recounts his experience tracing his efforts "to pass over to Buddhism." He describes this experience saying:

> . . . it has become clearer than ever that *Without Buddha I Could not be A Christian.* For me, not only does double-belonging seem to work. It is a necessity! The only way I can be religious is by being interreligious. I can be a Christian only by also being a Buddhist (2009:216).

Hick is convinced that his pluralist views will change theology in ways analogous to the way the Copernican revolution changed astronomy. The newer doctrines of pluralism will replace, he states, the older, outdated concepts of religion as the more accurate teachings of Copernicus replaced the inaccurate concepts of the Ptolemaic solar system. Hick defined the "Ptolemaic theology" as the system that insists on the principle that outside the Church, or Christianity, there is no salvation (1987: 125; 1987:16-35).

Pluralist Theology

Compared to exclusivists, and even inclusivists or Universalists, Pluralists refer less to definite biblical passages. These theologians do, however, maintain definite biblical and theological beliefs. The following theological positions characterize Pluralist theology.

Pluralists exalt the place of human reason in religious thinking. For Hick, human reason is the ultimate arbiter of truth and it is clear that the development of his work follows a trajectory determined by this evaluation according to reason. In terms of his arguments for universal salvation, his belief that this is the logical outcome of the creation of a loving God is central to the rest of his argument and indeed to the development of his theology (Hall 2011:401). The central place given to reason in Hick's viewpoints led to his rejection of most cardinal Christian doctrines. Of this tendency, Lindsay Hall writes:

> Hick is suggesting that these doctrines, if held in traditional forms, are incompatible with human reason.

Whilst he accepts that they may represent a general truth, human reason demands that belief in the miracles of Jesus and his physical resurrection, for example, be regarded as symbolic or spiritual rather than actual or physical events. For Hick, human reason is the ultimate arbiter of truth and it is clear that the development of his work follows a trajectory determined by this evaluation according to reason. In terms of his arguments for universal salvation, his belief that this is the logical outcome of the creation of a loving God is central to the rest (2011:403).

The centralization reason over revelation lies at the heart of much of what Evangelicals see as the basic problems of Pluralism.

Pluralists base revelation primarily on religious experience. They tend to replace propositional revelation with an epistemology that exalts the primacy of religious experience (see Paul Eddy 1993:26-38). Stress on religious experience leads Paul Knitter to declare that what is needed is not a Bible but a revelation that will allow every person's experience to be seen as valid. Knitter concludes, "The more the truth of my religion opens me to others, the more I can affirm it as absolute" (1985: 217-23). For Pluralists, the only universal standard rests in human experience and not in any particular sacred text or texts (see Ott, Strauss, and Tennent 2010: 299).

Many pluralists such as John Hick and Wilfred Cantwell Smith accept the experiential understanding of the individual as more important than any propositional truth. Religious traditions are true, they say, only as they impact and transform adherents of the system. No religious claim can ever be false since that claim is valid for those who follow a particular religion; no religion can be held as true and others as false (Pinnock 1988; Hick 1980b:173-74; 1980a:58). In the thinking of Hick, human reason is an essential and primary source for theology. He believes that the conservative evangelical tradition stifles the role of human reasoning (Hall 2011: 401). Hick reveals his view of revelation as he indicates that he does not consider the biblical revelation as either unique or superior. He writes:

> I thus see theology as a human creation. I do not believe that God reveals propositions to us, whether in

Only Jesus

Hebrew, Greek, English, or any other language. I hold that the formation of theology is a human activity that always, and necessarily, employs the concepts and reflects the cultural assumptions and biases of the theologian in question. As an example, the successive atonement doctrines that have become prominent during the history of Christian doctrine have reflected the statues of society within which they were produced (1995:36).

Pluralists believe the doctrine of Christ's historic Incarnation to be the product of myth. Hick recognizes that the biblical view of Christ would mean that: (1) only through Christ would any be saved; (2) that the large majority of the human race would not be saved; (3) and that pluralism would be destroyed. These realizations led Hick to conclude that the teaching of the Incarnation was the result of myth (see Hick 1995:29-59).

The early Christians, says Hick, were seeking to explain Jesus' unique impression and power, and made up the teaching of Incarnation. This mistaken notion led, says Hick, to the erroneous expressions of Nicea, the council at which Christians affirmed the deity of Christ. Based on this premise, Hick also questions other doctrines, such as Trinity, Atonement, and Resurrection. Hick's conclusion is that Jesus is not the only Savior but that God's salvation is available through many other religions and many other saviors (1973: 131, 171-81; 1982: 14; 1985: 34; 1995:51-57).

Hick calls upon Christians to move beyond their theological fundamentalism and literal interpretations of the Incarnation as Christianity has largely outgrown its literal belief in a six-day creation by God (see 1977:174; 184-84). Many Pluralists follow this thinking that sees the basic doctrines of Evangelical Christianity as myth and teach that good metaphors need not be taken as accurate or followed in a literal way (Hick 1995:89-91).

Pluralists believe salvation to be possible in all religions. The world religions provide salvation to the same degree as does Christianity. In fact, Hick and Knitter refer to the idea of "Christian uniqueness" as "myth" (1987). Moreover, Paul Knitter declares that the purpose of his edited book, T*he Myth of Religious Superiority,* is that of helping Christians to no longer insist that they have the only, or the final, or the superior path to God and absolute truth (2005: vii). In the thinking of Pluralists, *Christ is not the one and only way to salvation but one among many* (Hick and Knitter 1987:33). Hick and Knitter declare:

> What the pluralistic vision accordingly requires is not a radical departure from the diverse and ever-growing Christian tradition, but its further development in ways suggested by the discovery of God's presence and saving activity within other streams of human life. The resulting perception is that Christianity is not the one and only way of salvation, but one among several (1987, 33).

Roman Catholic Karl Rahner's view of "anonymous Christians" and "explict" and "anonymous" Christianity are other expressions of the theology of inclusivism/pluralism (Boutin 1983; 6-9). Paul Knitter declares Rahner, to be the most influential Catholic theologian of the 20th century. About Rahner, Knitter observed that while he spent most of his life in Germany and never studied other religions that his study of the Christian tradition, and his own deeply spiritual life, convinced him that God's world was much bigger than the Christian world. Rahner's creative and prodigious writings, says Knitter, were aimed at adding new lenses to the Christian telescope so that it could detect the active presence of God both deeply within the being of every human and through the expanse of history (2002:68). Knitter continued his glowing words about Rahner and his work pointing out that Rahner's lecture in 1961, that was later published as "Christianity and the Non-Christian Religions" in *Theological Investigations* (1966) constituted a truly revolutionary theology of religions (Ibid, 68).

According to Rahner's teachings, persons can become anonymous Christians *without ever hearing the name of Jesus* (1979:221). For Rahner an anonymous Christian is a person who through faith in God has entered into the company of the redeemed though not yet into the visible church (see, Chancellor 1994:541). People from all religions, polytheists, atheists, or pantheists can experience God's grace. Saving faith, says Rahner, comes through a Christ they do not know and yet can be enjoyed even when the person is not conscious of the realities that make him/her a Christian (1980:75-79).

Rahner contends that it is not sufficient to simply concede that values are found in the world's religions. It is necessary that Christianity recognize that the religions are historically tangible expressions of God's universal salvific will. Rahner believes that we can speak of the presence of the grace of Christ outside of Christianity and that "anonymous Christians" live in Hinduism, Islam, and Buddhism (see Rahner 1961:5:115-34 and the interpretation by Conn 1991:200).

In Rahner's viewpoint, God holds out his salvation to peoples around the world who are living after Christ yet actually living in a state as if Christ had not come. They live in the condition of Jewish people before Christ (see discussion in Ott, Strauss, Tennet 2010:298-99). For Pluralists, Christians and believers may not be the same and often are not the same.

Rahner, while admitting that other religions contain errors, believes they are vehicles of salvation because God mediates his offer, however, imperfectly, through them. The other religions are not equal to Christianity. Christians should confront adherents to other religions as anonymous Christians already touched by God's grace and truth (1966-1968: V:122; VI:390-98).

Obviously, Karl Rahner, with his concept of "anonymous Christians," upholds pluralism. He affirms both God's saving presence in other religions and Christ as the definitive and authoritative revelation of God (1966-83:312; 1980:75-80). Sanders declares that Rahner goes too far in his position and refers to Mikka Ruokanen who supports Pinnock's position as being more in line with Vatican II than Rahner's (Sanders 1994:45-48; Ruokanen 1992).

Rahner believes that when Christianity is introduced, these extra-Christian religions cease to be valid. Still, he holds that God's grace can be mediated through other religions (Ibid V:122). Hans Küng, another Catholic theologian, affirms the finality of Christ but at the same time believes salvation possible through the religions (1966; 109-61).

The findings of Vatican II accept most of Rahner's and Küng's conclusions (Ott, Strauss, Tennent 2010: 298). In *Gaudium et Spes* Vatican II declared that since God offers the possibility of Salvation to every person the Church should endorse the belief that the Holy Spirit in a mystery offers to every person this salvation. Vatican II, however, falls short of officially accepting Rahner's idea of "anonymous Christians." Vatican II did follow Rahner's lead in seeing "profound religious sense" in the other religious systems (Hinduism, Buddhism, Islam, and Traditional Religions).

These religions, says Vatican II, represent what is true and holy and reflect a ray of the Truth that enlightens all people. For these reasons, Vatican II urges Catholics to prudently and lovingly engage followers of other religions in discussion and dialogue. To a large degree, Vatican II sees in the other religions "elements of grace and truth" (See Knitter2002:75-77;
http//www.vatican.va/archieve/hist_councils/ii_vatican-council/documents/vat-ii_cons_19651207_gaudium-et-spes_en.html).

Vatican II while approaching many Pluralist teachings does not go so far as actually declaring the religions as paths to salvation. Bishop Piero Rossano explains that Vatican II does not indicate that salvation can reach people through the various religions (1981:102-103). The truth does stand, however, that Karl Rahner and Vatican II tend toward the basic teachings of Pluralism. These writers, however, are less committed to Pluralism than John Hick, William Hocking, Paul Knitter, William Cantwell Smith, Langdon Gilkey, and Tom F. Driver.

Pluralists believe in a salvation-centered Christianity.
They conceive salvation to be a response to the Real or Ultimate so that the responder is transformed from self-centeredness to Reality-centeredness. Paul Knitter thinks that this view of salvation calls for a radical reinterpretation of Jesus as less than the normative savior (Knitter 1985:143). It is not enough, he says, to believe that all people will be saved in the lifeboat of Christ—all people have their own lifeboats.

Hick further says that only God can create a human into a child of God, but different religions have their own names for God who acts to save them (Hick 1980:181; see discussion of this view in Sanders 1992:115-16). Hick more fully describes his viewpoint saying:

Only Jesus

The path of thought, reflecting both personal observation and a fair amount of reading, suggests to me that we should think of salvation in more universal terms than has been customary in Christian theology. This in turn leads to a new understanding of the function of the world religions, including Christianity. If we define salvation as being forgiven and accepted by God because of Jesus' death on the cross, then it becomes a tautology that Christianity alone knows and is able to preach the source of salvation. But if we define salvation as an actual human change, a gradual transformation from natural self-centeredness (with all the human evils that follow from this) to a radically new orientation centered in God and manifested in the "fruit of the Spirit," than it seems clear that salvation is taking place within all of the world religions—and taking place so far as we can tell, to more or less the same extent. On this view, which is not based on theological theory but on the observable realities of human life, salvation is not a juridical transaction inscribed in heaven, nor it iit a future hope beyond this life (although it is this too), but is a spiritual, moral, and political change that can begin now and whose present possibility in grounded in the structure of reality (1995:43).

Pluralists speak of the unknowable and unknown God. Hick's view of Scripture and the philosophy of Immanuel Kant led to the Pluralist's that the real God, the noumenal God, appears to people in various religions in ways that are both different and conflicting—both misleading and inadequate.

From this view, Hick came to believe that God is both unknown and unknowable. Every description of God only shows how the Real affects different people in different religious traditions. The Real is how humans subjectively discern the Real. Thus, Pluralists believe that the Real is involved in all authentic religions (Hick 1993: 158-59; 171).

Pluralists call for dialogue between the religions. The call for dialogue among pluralists goes beyond a mere call for discussion to a vital and necessary procedure to seek religious agreement. By dialogue Pluralists mean an encounter of religious persons on the level of their understandings of their deepest commitments and ultimate concerns, that is, their religious beliefs and positions (Swearer 1977:35).

Klaus Klostermaier explains that dialogue is more than an exchange of views between teachers of different religions. Such exchange, he says, is comparative religion not dialogue. Dialogue moves beyond interreligious meeting to persons meeting with a profound recognition of their mutuality (Klostermaier 1967: 119; 1971: 20).

Paul Knitter expresses his conviction in the imperative nature of interreligious dialogue. He goes further to declare that this dialogue needs and should be affiliated with liberation theology and its agendas. Such dialogue, says Knitter, can protect the Christian movement from developing ideology that would lead to seeking to promote one's own interest at the expense of others. The hermeneutics of suspicion that can develop in dialogue protects Christianity and others from this tendency to use doctrine to oppress others (1987:181-84).

Timothy Tennent expresses his lack of favor with much of what is taught by those who champion interreligious dialogue. He points out the many involved in cries for dialogue stem from the liberal side of Christian persuasion. Tennent notes that most approaches to dialogue insist that participants in dialogue suspend their own faith commitments before beginning the discussion. Secondly, proponents of dialogue declare that before the discussion can begin, participants should discard any convictions that absolute truth exists. Finally, these proponents of dialogue, says Tennent, demand that the "c" word, conversion, be ruled out of the discussions (2002:11-16). The evangelical view of dialogue is summed up in the statement, "We are called to be witnesses of Jesus Christ, even in the context of interreligious dialogue" (Ott, Strauss, Tennent 2010:314).

Indicating the accuracy of Tennent's first point in the preceding paragraph, Pluralism contends that true dialogue demands as one condition that the one engaging in religious dialogue approach the effort by being *engaged by the faith of the othe*r (Swearer 1977:40). Dialogue to be authentic must contain little or no predetermined expectations, total honesty, complete openness, and the untethered willingness to change even central beliefs and practices (see Pierson 2000:274-75).

John Cobb Jr. teaches that Christians who desire to engage in true dialogue with followers of other religions should not assume the superiority of their own experience and convictions but rather develop the trait of becoming eager to learn from others (2002:23). Approaching dialogue from the viewpoint that our conception of religion is the only true doctrine makes true dialogue impossible. This approach also, according to advocates of dialogue produces staleness in our own religiousness and the truncating of our own religious growth (Swearer 1977:41).

Stanley J. Samartha strongly attacks the conservative Evangelical concept that dialogue is a means of communicating the Christian message to followers of other religions. Speaking of the truth of Christianity, the falsities of the non-Christian religions, and the absoluteness and finality of Jesus Christ is the instrumental use of dialogue rather than the true way of establishing new relationship (1987:71-72). Panikkar contends that in the present dialogue, many Christians no longer want to conquer nor even convert but to serve, learn, and offer themselves as sincere participants in the open dialogue (1987: 95).

This free dialogue in which Christians are expected to open themselves to other religions and consider the possibility of accepting the claims of other religions is basic to the approach of pluralism (see Pierson 2000:274). While the call for dialogue is not actually a part of pluralist theology, it does represent such a central tendency of the teaching that the concept should be considered a basic building block in the movement.

Pluralism obviously follows a detailed and extensive theological agenda. The theology of Pluralism must be examined carefully from an Evangelical perspective.

An Evangelical Evaluation of Pluralism

Evangelicals recognize and appreciate the Pluralists' concern for the unevangelized and their desire to include all humans in God's salvation. Pluralists have, however, in the minds of Evangelicals, gone too far in trying to uphold their views. In attempting to establish the more open, wider, way to salvation, pluralists have affirmed what evangelicals consider unbiblical tenets (see Ott, Strauss, Tennent 2010: 302-303). An evaluation of Pluralism would incorporate the following conclusions.

The Pluralist model basically overlooks the truth of the Scriptures, as the Word of God. Evangelicals insist on the importance of the objective, propositional revelation found in the inspired Scripture. Pluralists place too much stress on the subjective, experiential aspects of revelation. They allow human experience to be the final and most comprehensive arbiter of all truth.

Evangelicals contend that Pluralism is a postmodern universalism that promotes relativism but does not produce unity. Pluralism employs a radical hermeneutic that dismisses objective truth in the effort to set the world of politics and religion on equal footing. The result is that in the effort to avoid any teaching of the superiority of any one group the salvation plan of God is reduced to socially constructed sincerity (see Stewart 2000:378).

Evangelicals hold the written revelation of the Bible in high regard and as the infallible Word of God. Scripture, not human logic, provides the source of our understanding of God and his will for humanity. The written Word, the Bible, is the perfect guide for belief and conduct—telling us what we should believe and what we should do. The Bible never misleads us in either of these pursuits.

The Pluralist model does not present a realistic understanding of Deity. Pluralist John Hick does not use the term, "God" but instead speaks of the "Real." This "ultimate reality" is so vague and uncertain that Hick thinks it can encompass the theism of Judaism and Islam as well as the non-theistic conceptions of Buddhism and Taoism. The result is basically a lack of a clear perception of Jehovah, God (see Ott, Strauss, Tennent 2010: 303).

Exclusivists maintain faith in a personal, living God, all-powerful and of infinite love. The infinite love of God does not, however, cancel God's ultimate resistance to all things sinful and evil. What God does and says is correct. Evangelicals follow the biblical teachings concerning God and his character and actions. Pluralist's teachings simply do not reach the level of biblical understandings of the Creator and

Savior Deity of the Bible.

The Pluralist model calls for the surrender of absolutes clearly taught in Scripture. Hick's later works advocate an understanding of salvation that seems to have no connection with an understanding of salvation based on the triumph of Christ over death (Hall 2011:415). In relation to the surrender of absolutes, Hick calls for eradication of Christian core tenets. He states that many Christian teachings are, in the opinions of many theologians today including his own, either quite untenable or open to serious doubt. The list includes *creatio ex nihilo*, the physical resurrection of Jesus, atonement, the fall, and the miracles of Jesus (1973:92).

The surrender of Christian absolutes in Pluralistic teachings is nowhere more apparent than in teachings of the eternal state. Of the doctrine of Hell, Hick repeats the often-heard statement, "The doctrine of hell has as its implied premise either that God does not desire to save all His human creatures, in which case He is only limitedly good, or that His purpose has finally failed in the case of some . . . in which case He is only limitedly sovereign" (1973:419). He continues this line of thinking, "who can believe that God condemns the majority of the human race, who have never encountered or have not accepted the Christian gospel, to eternal damnation. Personally I would view such a God as the Devil!" (1995:19). Finally, Hick dismisses the Christian concept of eternal punishment, saying, "no finite human sin could justly deserve an infinite punishment, and second, such retribution could never serve a good purpose—compatible with the limitless love of God—because, being endless, it could never lead to the eventual restoration of the sinner" (1999:68).

Evangelicals insist on maintaining doctrines such as the reality and Triune nature of God, the historical and divine Christ, the inspired and truthful Bible, the Death and Resurrection of Christ, salvation that involves freeing sinful humanity from the alienation caused by sin, the possibility of Salvation in Christ *and in him alone,* and the reality of the eternal separation of the lost from God. Pluralists, it seems, are willing to sacrifice any of these basic truths in their search for salvation in any religion. The Manila Declaration observes that "Pluralism gives too much authority to relativistic views of revelation, denying Christianity's witness to

God's non-relativistic action in the world in Jesus Christ" (1992:15).

Carl Braaten concludes his critique of Pluralism showing that Pluralism does not make clear the meaning of salvation. In pluralistic teachings, the basic meaning of salvation is clouded becoming any number of things, such as illumination, equality, physical health, peace, or justice. The failure of Pluralism, according to Braaten, is that it fails to show that salvation deals with the fundamental alienation of humanity with God (1981:69-72). Until salvation is demonstrated to deal with this alienation (lostness), all other aspects of salvation "remain ultimately cosmetic" (1994:40).

The Pluralist model communicates a wider-hope for salvation that is not promised in revealed truth. The teachings of Pluralism may provide a message of safety in the "religions" that does not exist. The wider-hope may well be too wide. Pluralism may promise salvation in places where no salvation lies. Evangelicals hold this truth.

Sinclair B. Ferguson has insightfully written:

> But in fact all Scripture allows us to say is that we cannot assume that any who have never heard the gospel will be saved. We must recognize that what God may do is not limited to what he has revealed to us that he will do. But by the same token we may not presume that he will do what he has not specially revealed that he will do (2004:236).

Evangelicals will not promise more than God has promised nor hold out hope that the Lord in his gracious revelation has not established. The Evangelical message continues to state that if ways to salvation other than through faith in Jesus Christ exist, the Bible has not revealed anything about them.

The Pluralist model conceives of persons becoming Christian apart from special revelation or Christian experience. This concept is expressed in terms of "anonymous Christians" or "pagan saints." Most evangelicals cannot accept the concept of a difference between Christians and believers ("anonymous Christians" or "pagan saints"). Evangelicals have problems with Pluralists and Inclusivists in regard to these teachings. Some Evangelicals contend that Rahner teaches that the Church and the sacraments are mysteriously embodied in the communities that gather in the temples or the mosques and thus provide salvation (see Ott, Strauss, Tennent 2010:305).

Exclusivists do not accept the idea that the Bible teaches that some people have come to Christ on the basis of general revelation. Pluralists point to non-Jewish people mentioned in the Bible as followers of God such as Melchesdick, Rahab, Caleb). Exclusivists think that it is far more likely that these "holy pagans" were all responding to God's special revelation given in their own periods of time (Ott, Strauss, Tennent 2010: 313-140). Christopher Little concludes that the non-Jewish, Old Testament persons who came to saving faith all received special revelation which led to their reconciliation with God (2000:88).

The Pluralist model finds salvation outside of faith in Jesus Christ. Hick dismisses the uniqueness of Christ because of the scandal of particularity (Hall 2011:405). In fact, Hick argues that, "given a faith in the universal saving activity of God, it is impossible to hold that salvation is only for those living within one particular strand of history, namely the Judaic-Christian strand" (1968:74). Hick on the basis of his commitment to reason rejects the Incarnation and the Resurrection of Christ (Hall 2011:408-409). Little wonder that he does not affirm salvation in Christ alone.

Exclusivists accept Jesus Christ as the one and only way to salvation. They can find no believable teaching in Scripture to indicate that any way exists to bring followers of other religions into the same fold as believers. The position of Exclusivists rests on the biblical doctrine of the uniqueness of Christ as the one and only way to come into right-standing with God (see Ott, Strauss, Tennent 2010:318).

Acts 4:12 clearly presents Jesus Christ as the one and only way to salvation. Peter emphasizes that this uniqueness of Jesus Christ was delivered to Jewish people who were certainly religious—but not saved people. There is simply no other place for salvation in Christ. Jesus is the absolutely unique Savior who alone provides salvation for humans who trust Him. Jesus claimed that no one came (or comes) to the Father except by him (John 14:6) (see Murray 2005:28-30;

Cate 2005:37-68).

Evangelicals must realize that this present day with relativism and tolerance so highly valued and faithfully practiced, they must hold to the absolute that salvation is found in Jesus Christ and in him only. They must also accept the fact that such convictions will not be popular. All roads do not lead up to the identical top of the same mountain. Without pride or arrogance, God's people must remain firmly committed to the truth that Jesus Christ is the unique savior and that only byfaith in him during lifetime can one reach the place of eternal life (see Cate 2005:46-50; Ott, Strauss, Tennent 2010: 318-24).

The major problem with pluralism stems from the failure to provide a proper place to the unique Christ in the human drama and salvation experience. The Manila Declaration, which rejects this viewpoint, defines pluralism as a way of thinking that sometimes merely describes the existing diversity among religions but often goes on to declare that all religious beliefs are "more-or-less equally valid and equally true and that all religious beliefs have a rough parity with one another" (1992:14). The writers of the WEF clearly summarize the findings relative to the uniqueness of Christ, saying:

> . . . we affirm that Jesus Christ is the centre, ground, norm, and goal of all religious insight and knowledge. In addition we affirm that the universal message of Christ is essentially dependent on the historical Jesus Christ who, in his particularity, is the very act of God and that therefore it is not appropriate to refer to the Christian principle in other religions, or to the cosmic Christ, or to the hidden Christ, or the unnamed Christ except in connection with and in dependence on Jesus of Nazareth (1992:26).

Chris Wright beautifully summarizes the truth about the uniqueness of Jesus Christ saying:

> The uniqueness of Jesus is not something Christians invented. It is a truth which has been entrusted to us as stewards and witnesses. The final proof of it rests with God himself who, meanwhile, has exalted him to the highest place and given him his own supreme name (1994:44).

Only Jesus

The Pluralist model concedes too much in the efforts to achieve dialogue. Evangelicals stand willing to engage in dialogue with leaders of other religions. In this dialogue, Christians should not set aside their biblically based beliefs. They should not set aside their ultimate goal of conversion (see Netland 1995:265-66). Timothy Tennent is right on point saying:

> In short, I take a different point of departure when it comes to the evangelistic side of dialogue. Rather than viewing conversion as taboo, I fully expect Muslim or Hindus or Buddhist to do their bests to convince me that they have more coherent worldviews and clearer visions of God or reality than the Christian faith has. Likewise, I am free to make the best case I can for the Christian gospel, realizing that in the end I may remain the only convinced Christian. One the other hand, there is the possibility that I or one the other participants may become convinced by the compelling truth of Christianity or Islam or Hinduism. It is unprincipled to rule out from the start the possibility of conversion, since the very nature of the dialogue assumes we are discussing weighty matter of life-changing significance (2002:16).

Alan R. Tippett approaches dialogue with the question concerning the possibilities that the dialogue will allow the witness to persuade persons to the Christian point of view and to experience with Christ. He expresses his concern that in dialogue Christians might surrender basic truth. Tippett writes:

> I am not denying that there may be some truth in the Koran and the Upanishads, but for me as a Christian missionary my norm is the Bible. I am ready to read the sacred books of the people to whom I go, because they help me to understand them better as people, to know why they behave as they do, and to learn to speak their language. I want to identify with them, to be sympathetic and to help them in any way I can. I shall endeavour [sic] to be humble as I present the truth in Christ. I might even learn some truth which sends me back to the Bible to something I had not noticed before, but when I am called to mission, I am sent to proclaim and to make-disciples. I have not received a research grant to see what truth that lies in Islam speaks to us (1969:41).

Tippett explains that Particularists should keep in mind that we dialogue in order to convert. We are following the Commission to make disciples. Exclusivists in the proper effort to understand and be understood must not in the name of dialogue surrender basic truths of the faith. This truth is echoed by David Bosch who contributes these words:

> We know only in part, but we do know. And we believe that the faith we profess is both true and just, and should be proclaimed. We do this, however, not as judges or lawyers, but as witnesses; not as soldiers, but as envoys of peace; not as high-pressure salespersons, but as ambassadors of the Servant Lord (1991:489).

This statement provides the best foundation for dialogue in Christian relationship with and witness to the followers of the other religions.

Conclusion

In summary, Evangelicals find it impossible to accept what they consider unbiblical views such as the subjective view of revelation, the relativistic view of God, the rejection of the Christian doctrines of Incarnation, Trinity, the Deity of Christ, Atonement, and Christ as the one and only Savior. "Evangelicals persist in their views of the necessity of biblical revelation, the deity of Christ, the finality of Christ's Work, and the truth that salvation comes only by explicit faith in the explicit message of Christ" (Smith 1998:419). Evangelicals, therefore, must reject the Pluralist answer that sees salvation in all religions.

Exclusivists see no biblical promise of salvation apart from personal faith in the historic Christ, his atoning death, and victorious resurrection. Hearing the cry of Pluralists, and applauding their commitment to all peoples and all religions, Exclusivists remain in their convictions as to the uniqueness of the revelation in Christ and the salvation promised in and only in his name. The message of lostness (separation from the Eternal God) brings grief, sadness, and terror to Christian hearts. It is, however, to the biblical teaching of the eternal separation of the unrepentant that Exclusivists remain committed.

Only Jesus

The Exclusivist conclusion remains that belief in and experience with the historic Christ during a person's lifetime provides the path to salvation as presented in the Bible. This view is accompanied not by any pride or feeling of superiority but in heartbreak for those who remain outside the eternal hope in Christ in the state of having no hope in the world (Eph 2:1-10).

CHAPTER 4

THE INCLUSIVIST
APPROACH

A third wider-hope approach, Inclusivism, affirms not only the particularity and finality of salvation in Christ but also teaches that people can and will find Christ in other religions, or in general revelation, or through God's providence. D. A. Carson, who certainly does not affirm Inclusivism, defines it as ". . . the view that all who are saved are saved on account of the person and work of Jesus Christ, but that conscious faith in Jesus Christ is not absolutely necessary: some may be saved by him who have never heard of him, for they may respond positively to the light they have received" (1996: 278-79).

Paul Knitter calls this view the "New Fulfillment Model." He writes that the Replacement Model (exclusivism, particularism) may have "held sway over" most groups in Christian history. He continues, however, stating that this "fulfillment model" *is not* only the view of the theologians in the mainline churches but also the belief of theologically informed Christians in these churches (2002:63).

Knitter contends that the Fulfillment Model (inclusivism) represents the teachings of today's mainline churches such as the Lutheran, Reformed, Methodist, Anglican, Greek Orthodox, and Roman Catholic Churches. He continues saying that "They [the leaders and members of these church groups] believe that other religions are of value that God is to be found in them, that Christians need to dialogue with them and not just preach to them" (Ibid 63). These new understandings, concludes Knitter, calls for a new theology of religions (ibid).

Most Inclusivists acknowledge that Jesus Christ is the definitive and authoritative revelation of God and that Christ's work on the Cross is central in that no one saved apart from this work. They differ from Exclusivists in their contention that there must be a universal access to the gospel and that a personal knowledge of and response to Christ is not necessary for salvation (Sanders 1992:60-62; 131-37; 216-17; See evaluation of Inclusivism by Geivett 2000: 112).

Inclusivists also contend that the religions have some sort of saving power (Kittner 2005:188-90). In fact, Pinnock declares McGrath to be an Exclusivist rather than in Inclusivism because McGrath "sees no saving value in other religions" (1995:188). Advocates of Inclusivism contend that if every human has been provided redemption in Jesus Christ then it must be possible for every person to be able to receive that provision (Hackett 1984:244). Universal access to the Gospel and saving value in the religions are absolutes among Inclusivists (Sanders 1992: 1992-93).

Those who never hear the gospel, say Inclusivists, may still attain salvation in at least two ways (1) if they respond to God's general revelation before they die or (2) through postmortem encounter (Sanders 1995:22-46). They deny that knowledge of Christ's work is necessary for salvation (Sanders 1992: 215). Vatican statements declare that persons who do not know the Gospel of Christ or his Church through no fault of their own can attain everlasting salvation by the fact they are moved by grace and strive by their deeds to do God's will as they are led by their consciences (LG 16). Inclusivists answer the question, "Is Jesus the Only Savior?" with a "Yes, but . . . (Nash 1994: 9).

In summary, Sanders teaches that inclusivism boasts a broader support in the Church today than any other wider-hope theory. He holds, in error I think, that inclusivism is gaining support among many evangelicals—including some from even the fundamentalist groups. Sanders claims that inclusivism is today the dominant view among Roman Catholics and is beginning to challenge restrictivism within evangelical circles (1992:216-17, 274).

The Basic Concepts
of Inclusivism

Inclusivism contends that salvation is possible in non-Christian religions and in general revelation yet still affirms Christ as God's definitive and authoritative revelation (see Gavin D'Costa 1986:81). These theologians prefer what they call a "universality axiom," which sees salvation as open to all over the "particularity axiom," which focuses on Christ and the unique and final savior (Pinnock 1988: 153, 157).

The Inclusivist Approach

A leading spokesperson, Clark Pinnock defines inclusivism as "the view upholding Christ as the Savior of humanity but also affirming God's saving presence in the wider world and in other religions" (1992:15). While differing in emphases, the statements of the writers who follow inclusivism in some way point to the possibility of finding salvation other than in Christ alone. John Sanders explains that the unevangelized are saved or lost on the basis of their commitment, or lack thereof, to the God who saves through Jesus Christ. Salvation can be received through general revelation and God's providential workings in history. Inclusivism admits that salvation is only in Christ but denies that knowledge of him is necessary. The work of Jesus is ontologically necessary in that no one can be saved without it. The Work of Christ is, however, not epistemologically necessary as one need not be aware of Christ's work to benefit from it (1992: 215).

Sanders expresses these views clearly:

> Some advocates of the wider hope maintain that some of those who never hear the gospel of Christ may nevertheless attain salvation before they die if they respond in faith to the revelation they do have. Proponents of this position—which I will be referring to as *inclusivism*—contend that the unevangelized are saved or lost on the basis of their commitment, or lack thereof, of to the God who saves through the work of Jesus. They believe that appropriation of salvic grace is mediated through general revelation and God's providential workings in human history. Briefly, inclusivists affirm the particularity and finality of salvation only in Christ but deny that knowledge of his work is necessary for salvation. That is to say, they hold that the work of Jesus is ontologically necessary for salvation (no one would be saved without it) but not epistemologically necessary (one need not be aware of the work in order to benefit from it). Or in other words, people can receive the gift of salvation without knowing the giver or the precise nature of the gift (1992:215).

A variety of positions exists within the inclusivist camp. To understand inclusivism, one must consider both the groups' biblical interpretations and theological formulations.

Biblical Interpretation and Inclusivism

More than Pluralists, Inclusivists base their views on what Sanders calls "a wealth of evidence . . . in the Bible" (1992: 132). Clark Pinnock interprets Genesis 1-11 in the context of God's concern for all the world. He believes the covenant with Noah (Gen. 9:8-17) shows God as, not a tribal deity, but One who extends salvation to all. Pinnock teaches that God's call to Abram and the event of Genesis 10 both reveal God's desire to be Savior for all. Pinnock concludes, "any attempt to present God's saving plan on a small scale is on the wrong track and misses the point of early Genesis" (1992:20-21).

Sanders concurs saying that God's universal saving intention cannot be derailed by race nor geography because the God of Abraham desires that all be saved (1 Tim 2:4, 2 Pet 3:9, 1 Tim 4:10). "God has not left the human race," says Sanders, "to fear and alienation but has provided redemption through his beloved Son." God is willing to save even those who have rejected and hurt him (Isa 55:7) (1992:133).

Sanders says that God sought to bring Pharaoh to him by the plagues in Egypt (Exo 7:5, 17, 8:10). He points to the account of Jonah as indicating God's desire for those outside of Israel (1995:22-35). Pinnock interprets Psalms 87:4 and 47:1, 8-9 as teaching that God chose Israel for the sake of the world. He says, "Although Israel is certainly central in the Old Testament narrative, we should not miss the frequent texts that remind us of God's interest in the wide world as well" (1992:27-28).

Inclusivists contend that the universality of God's salvation occupies a central place in Jesus' proclamation of the Kingdom as seen in his promises of mercy and boundless grace (Luke 18:9-14, 15:11-15, 15:6). In fact, Pinnock sees the unlimited mercy of God and the theme of hope as distinguishing marks of Jesus' message (1992: 30-31). Israel and the Gentiles both have a part in God's Kingdom. Pinnock thinks that those mentioned in Matt 10:15, 11:22, 12:41-42 show God's wider grace. "Jesus," says Pinnock, "does not want a house full, but a house filled" (Luke 14:23)

(1992:31-32).

God's mercy in his dealings with persons and nations from non-Israelites in the pre-Abrahamic period, according to Pinnock, shows the wider-scope of divine salvation. Persons such as Abel, Enoch, Balaam, the Queen of Sheba, and even Ruth give evidence of God's favor on people outside the Abrahamic covenant. Moreover, say Iinclusivists, Gentiles such as Jethro, Rahab, and Naaman are mentioned favorably in Scripture. Of particular significance in the thinking of inclusivists is Melchizedek, described as a Canaanite god called *El Elyon* (Gen 14:17-24). These ideas guide Pinnock to suggest there were believers outside Israel who contributed to God's plan (1992:26). Pinnock concludes saying:

> Let me sketch the way I see inclusivism to be congruent with the Scriptures. In the Old Testament, Melchizedek is an important symbol (Gen 14:17-24). The story of his encounter with Abram shows that God was at work in the religious sphere of Canaanite culture. Abram accepts the blessing of this pagan priest and pays tithes to him. He is satisfied that the king of Salem worships the true God under the name *El Elyon.* God seems to be teaching Abram that his election does not mean that he is in exclusive possession of God, but rather that God is calling him to be a means of grace to all nations among whom God is also and already at work. Melchizedek represents for me the larger group of pagan saints in Scripture among whom God worked. For too long we have stared at the corrupt forms of religion mentioned in the Bible as if they represented the fullness of what religion can be according to the Scripture, when there is more to it than that (1995: 109).

Inclusivists understand the experience of Jesus with the centurion (Matt 8:10) as teaching that the Roman had faith. Sanders writes, "Although his understanding was not theologically developed, it was commended for its existential quality" (1992:221). The account of Cornelius (Acts 10) is also interpreted by Inclusivists to teach that Cornelius was saved before Peter came to him, by his faith not his works of fearing God and doing good (Sanders 1992:223). Pinnock, who terms the account of Cornelius "a key symbol," (1995:109) says that those like Cornelius who now have faith in God, wherever they live, are accepted by God in the same way as Abraham, on the basis of their faith (1992:96).

Only Jesus

Texts often used by particularists to substantiate the view of pessimism and exclusivism are, in inclusvists' thinking taken out of context. In this line of reasoning, Pinnock writes:

> A Trinitarian theology supplies the broad and adequate basis we need for openness and hope. Those tests used to support pessimism and exclusivism are being read out of context. Of course there is on other name given to us by which to be saved (Acts 4:12), but Peter is referring to messianic salvation including physical healing through Jesus' name. He is not denying premessianic occurrences of God's grace. Certainly Jesus is the way, the truth, and the life, and no one comes to the Father but by him (Jn 14). No one else can show us the way to find God understood as Abba, Father. But in saying this, Jesus is not denying the trough about the Logos enlightening everyone coming into the world (Jn 1:9). He is not denying God at work in the wider world beyond Palestine and before his own time (1992:78).

An interpretation of these "exclusivists" passages that is offered by inclusivists claims that these scriptures, especially Act 4:12 and John 14:6 do not speak of the unevangelized (Sanders 1992;62-64). Pinnock declares that Acts 4:12 does not demand an exclusivists interpretation. It does not, he contends, deny eschatological salvation to most of the people who ever lived on earth, a view that he stresses he considers "utterly repugnant" (1991:112).

In general, inclusivists interpret Paul's words to the people in Lystra (Acts 14:156-17) to mean that these people already possessed truth from God in the context of their religion. Likewise, the account of the Apostle with the Athenian philosophers (Acts 17:28-30) indicates, to inclusivists, that God had revealed himself to the people in Greek culture and that Paul acknowledged the authenticity of the Athenians' worship of their unknown God (Pinnock 1988;158; 1992:96). John Sanders interprets these accounts to show that God has not left himself without witness in the other religions (1992:260; see also Sanders 1988:247-48). Pinnock declares his conclusion in regard to these pivotal passages saying, "The breath of God is free to blow wherever it wills (Jn 3:8) . . . There is no hint of the grace of God being limited to a single thread of human history" (1992:78).

Sanders interprets these biblical texts as teaching that all who respond to the revelation they have by calling out to God will be saved by Jesus Christ, since calling out to God is, in fact, calling upon the Lord Jesus (1992:68).

Pinnock, with other inclusivists, believes that Paul in Romans is more optimistic about the salvation of the "nations" than many interpreters allow. He admits that Paul stresses the failure of sinners to respond to God and that no person can save himself apart from God's redemptive Work. "But," says Pinnock, "it is wrong to read into his words in Romans the idea that he is denying that many Jews and Gentiles in the past have responded positively to God on the basis of this light, as Luke also intimates in the book of Acts" (1992:33).

Inclusivists use the Revelation and John's vision of the transformed world (Rev. 21:5) to bolster their position. They understand the picture of the kings of the earth bringing the glory and honor of their nations to God (Rev 21: 24-26) as teaching that nothing from these cultures will be lost.   Pinnock asks, "How could the One who is 'king of the ages,' who created the whole world, and whose throne is surrounded by Noah's rainbow, not have a purpose for the whole creation or be content to rescue a pathetic remnant (Rev 15:3; 10:6; 4:3)" (1992: 35). Inclusivists take seriously the promise, "All nations will come and worship before you, for your righteous acts have been revealed" (Rev 15:4). Using these passages, Pinnock concludes, "the Bible itself closes with an eloquently portrayed optimism of salvation" (1992: 35).

Obviously, Inclusivists use and honor Scripture. For this stand, Exclusivists respect them. Evangelicals think, however, that many of the interpretations from inclusivist writers fail to conform to accurate and overall biblical interpretations. In addition, particularists think that inclusivists stand on shaky ground and tend to explain away clear biblical statements where these are different from their inclusivitist views. This assessment will be clear as we turn to inclusivists' theology.

The Theology of Inclusivism

Inclusivist theology takes a middle ground between Pluralism and Exclusivism, but differs drastically from both. Inclusivist thinking not only highly evaluates other religions but in the words of Paul Knitter declares that the religions provide actual assistance in learning the true nature of Christian commitment. As seen earlier, Knitter declares that without Buddha he could not be a Christian (2009).

Inclusivism centralizes universally-accessible salvation. No teaching is more central among inclusivists than that salvation must be available to all, regardless of race, geography, or access to the Christian message. Sanders writes:

> According to the inclusivist view, the Father reaches out to the unevangeliszed through both the Son and the Spirit via general revelation, conscience and human culture. God does not leave himself without witness to any people. Salvation for the unevangelized is made possible only by the redemptive work of Jesus, but God applies that work even to those who are ignorant of the atonement. God does this if people respond in trusting faith to the revelation they have. In other words, unevangelized person may be saved on the basis of Christ's work if they respond in faith to the god who created them (1995a: 23-26, 36).

The view of universally-accessible salvation avoids, say inclusivists, the error that only a few will be saved and that of holding all will be saved. This inclusivist view springs from the conviction concerning the unbounded generosity of God (Pinnock 1992:17-18). Inclusivists insist that universal provision demands universal access and that while knowledge of Christ is not directly imperative (see, Ott, Strauss, Tennent 2010:297).

Sanders disputes the "fewness doctrine" that teaches that only a few will be saved but holds to his own view of a wider-hope. Stating that restrictivists base their views on passages such as Matt 7:13-14; Luke 13:23-30; and Matt 22:14, Sanders contends that the biblical texts support wider-hope thinking more than fewness thinking. His conclusion is:

The God of the Bible is utterly amazing: he includes all in his grace and excludes in judgment only those who spurn that grace. God has already accepted all people prior to an response on our part, but not all accept his acceptance. The saved respond in faith to the manifold graces of God, while the damned reject them. Because of the work of Christ, God accept all. Only those who decline to accept God grace are rejected (1995a:33).

Inclusivism insists that the doctrine of universally assessable salvation is biblical and correct and demands that this view be accepted. The doctrine of universally assessable salvation remains a pillar of inclusivism.

Another projected method of finding salvation possibilities and universally accessible salvation finds support in the concept of "Middle Knowledge" of God (see Sanders 1992: 167-71; 173-75). William Lane Craig defines Middle Knowledge of God as

God's knowledge of what every possible free creature would do under any possible set of circumstances and, hence, knowledge of those possible worlds which god can make actual. The content of this knowledge is not essential to God (1987: 131).

Craig attributes the concept of God's Middle Knowledge (*Scientia Media*) to the work of the Spanish Jesuit priest of the Counterreformation, Luis Molina (1535-1600). Craig is convinced that this concept of God's Middle Knowledge answers questions concerning divine providence, foreknowledge, and the situation of persons who never hear the gospel (1989: 184-88).

Two theologians, Donald Lake and George Goodman accept the teaching of God's Middle Knowledge. They not only believe that God's salvation is universally accessible but also that those who would have accepted him had they heard of him will be saved even though they remain ignorant of direct teachings concerning him (Sanders 1992:168-69). Donald Lake declares:

A valid offer of grace has been made to mankind, but its application is limited by man's response rather than God's arbitrary selection. God knows who would, under ideal circumstance, believe the gospel, and on the basis of his foreknowledge, applies that gospel even if the person never hears the gospel during his lifetime (1999:43).

In Sanders' understanding of Goodman's view, if God can see that one would have responded if the light had reached that one, then the fact that this person did not hear the message would not prevent the outflow of God's grace to him or her (1992:169). Lake points to his understanding that the Atonement of Christ has universal dimensions and is not related only to the elect. He writes:

> . . . it is a fact that these redemptive events in the life of Jesus provided a salvation so extensive, so broad as to potentially include the whole of humanity past, present and future (1999:31).

One way of reaching this universal dimension of the Atonement is through the concept of God's Middle Knowledge.

William Craig, who has been recorded as accepting the teaching of God's Middle Knowledge, contends that the doctrine is helpful in considering the unevangelized. In a stand not supported by Goodman and Lake, Craig seems to think an act of faith is necessary for salvation (1989:1876-87; Sanders 1992:169; 173-75). Craig thinks that the number who might be saved though they do not hear the message of Christ will be small.

He does, however, open the door to the possibility of salvation through God's Middle Knowledge as he teaches that many who are not able to hear the message will be judged on the basis of their response to general revelation and the light they have. He says that any who are judged and condemned on the basis of their failure to respond to the light of general revelation cannot legitimately complain of unfairness for their condemnation due to having never heard of Christ since they would not have responded had they received special revelation. Craig concludes that God in his providence has so arranged the world that anyone who would receive Christ has the opportunity to do so. God loves all persons and desires the salvation of all. God, therefore, supplies sufficient grace for salvation to every individual and nobody who would receive Christ if he were to hear the gospel will be denied their opportunity (1989:186).

Sanders expresses some doubt that Craig is actually in the group that support the teachings of universally accessible salvation. Craig may be, says Sanders, a restrictivist trying to relieve God of responsibility for the failure to give all persons the opportunity of hearing the gospel. In the end, Sanders declares the position of Craig to be "unsatisfactory" (1992:174-75).

Pinnock, who himself does not endorse the idea of Middle Knowledge, expressed some positive response when he thought he heard a possibility of such thinking in the response of Geivett/Phillips to McGrath. Pinnock thought the glimmer of hope seen in ideas of Middle Knowledge would escape the dead end of soteriological restrictivism, which hope Pinnock would consider a positive matter (1995:144-45). While expressing some belief that God's Middle Knowledge might help in the understanding of the condition of the unevangelized, Pinnock makes clear his view that the concept cannot be adequately supported philosophically (Ibid, 145).

The idea of God's Middle Knowledge does provide one avenue for those who insist on universally accessible salvation to defend their positions. The view does not have great standing as most scholars, including Sanders and Pinnock, do not accept it as valid. The teaching does, however, give some idea that salvation might be available to all.

Inclusivism insists that in spite of the misunderstanding of some exclusivists, universally-accessible salvation will never be the same as universalism, as "C sharp will never become an E flat, or pink become red" (Knitter 1985:136). Inclusivists contend that correct biblical doctrine and adequate Christian proclamation will never be reached until it is admitted that *while all will not respond and be saved that every person has access to salvation.* In this statement one sees the vast divide between Universalism and Inclusivism.

Inclusivism maintains a difference between Christians and Believers. Sanders states categorically, "Inclusivists contend that all Christians are believers but that not all believers are Christians" (Sanders 1992: 225). Christians are, according to this view, believers who know about Jesus, his earthly ministry, and who participate in his work. Believers are persons who trust in God but without the explicit knowledge of Jesus Christ and can be termed "holy pagans" or "pagan saints" (Ibid.).

The source of salvation for both is the same, Christ's atonement but the salvation is attained through different channels (Sanders 1992:228). It is the personal reality of God known in personal relation that saves rather than knowledge about the historical Jesus, according to Dale Moody (1981:61). Attention has already been directed at Pinnock's views of persons outside the biblical revelation who were, he thinks, accepted by God. After long and detailed explanations of these "pagan" believers (1992:92-1060, Pinnock concludes:

> No one knows how many holy pagans there may be. Some missionaries tell me they have encountered people like Cornelius but not many. Others are more hopeful. But we are not in a position to know how many there are. Only God can know people's hearts responses to him. All we know for sure is that people are free to respond to God anywhere in the world, thanks to his grace. This encourages us to be open to the work of God in the wider world as we proclaim the gospel and encounter outsiders (1992:106).

Inclusivism believes salvation is possible through the Non-Christian religions. Jesus is the only Savior but his salvation can be found in other religions. On the matter of salvation through the non-Christian religions, Rahner and the Inclusivists are almost identical. Many writers include the teachings of Karl Rahner and Vatican II as Inclusivist doctrine (see Ott, Strauss, Tennent 2010:298-99). This book, the reader will remember, placed Rahner's materials among the Pluralists.

Inclusivist Raimundo Panikkar calls for an "authentically universal Christology." Persons are saved, says Panikkar, not by the sacraments of Christianity or by the sacraments of their own religions but by the "*musterion*" active in both religions. He believes Christ to be already at work within Hindu thought and faith. His goal is a healthy pluralism that does not dilute the particular contributions of any human tradition

(1981: 85-86; 1988:107-109). Panikkar, with other inclusivists, obviously sees the possibility of salvation in other religions.

Clark Pinnock does not seek to hide his acceptance of the possibilities of salvation in other religions. The religions are in his thinking "windows of opportunity" for the Spirit to engage people (1995:116). The decisive word from Pinnock's pen expresses his optimistic view. He writes, "I accept the doctrine of general or cosmic revelation, and I believe that may people in the other religions worship God, even if in ways that fall conceptually short of the revelation of God nature which Christ brings" (1992:46).

Inclusivism believes that salvation is possible through general revelation. Since general revelation has its source in God it can mediate and communicate his saving mercy. Revelation does not save but God saves through general revelation. Persons are saved or lost, say inclusivists, depending on their responses to general revelation (Sanders 1995: 42-43).

Both Clark Pinnock and John Sanders express intense belief in salvation in and through general revelation. The former writes, ". . . the knowledge of God is not limited to places where biblical revelation has penetrated" (1988:159). The latter makes clear his position and that of inclusivism writing:

> They [Inclusivists] believe that appropriation of salvific grace is mediated through general revelation and God's providential workings in human history. Briefly, inclusivists affirm the particularity and finality of salvation only in Christ but deny to say, they hold that the work of Jesus is ontologically necessary for salvation (no one would be saved without it) but not epistemologically necessary (one need not be aware of the work in order to benefit from it). Or in other words, people can receive the gift of salvation without knowing the giver or the precise nature of the gift (1992:215).

As already noted, Inclusivists see God's mercy in his dealings with non-Israelite persons and nations in the pre-Abrahamic period. They point to Abel, Enoch, Lot, Balaam, the Queen of Sheba, and Ruth as examples of persons on whom God's favor rested although they were not part of the

Abrahamic covenant. The Old Testament, say inclusivists, mentioned favorably Gentiles such as Jethro, Rahab, and Naaman and even praises the Canaanite priest, Melchizedek (Gen 14:17-24). Pinnock concludes that while Abram did have a special calling from God, other believers also contributed to and were part of God's plan (Pinnock 1992:26; Sanders 1988:257).

Inclusivists point to examples of God working outside the covenant with Israel to bring Gentiles to salvation. They point to Melchizedek, Rahab, the Ninevites (of Jonah's day), the Queen of Sheba, and Cornelius. They lean on statements such as God "has not left himself without testimony" (Acts 14:17) and that Gentiles have "the requirements of the Law . . . written on their hearts" (Rom 2:15) to teach that God has an independent witness that can and does bring people to salvation (For discussion of this belief, see Ott, Strauss, Tennent 2010:298). Clearly, Inclusivists contend that salvific grace is brought through general revelation as well as special revelation.

Many Inclusivists, and some not in the inclusivist camp, have inferred some confidence in what they call implicit-faith as they seek an answer to the question of the condition of those who do not hear the message of salvation. The essence of the implicit-faith view is the belief that in some way, even outside of special revelation, there exists a means for salvation of lost humans. This view contends that in cultures that have no contact with the open message of Christ God prompts people to cast themselves into his hands for safe keeping.

People who hold "implicit faith" are convinced that people are saved through God's divine mercy. They are saved objectively on the basis of Christ's atonement. They are saved subjectively in that God elicits a faith response to the glimmer of light in natural revelation (general revelation). They believe that only Jesus is Savior but deny that one must know about Jesus to be saved (for description of implicit-faith theology, see David Clark 1991 41-44; Also see, Pinnock 1988:152-68; 1995; 108-112).

In bolstering the concept of implicit-faith, Pinnock makes much of this view that he calls the "Melchizedek Factor" (Gen 14:17-24). He points out that when Abraham, the father of the faith of Israel, met Melchizedek, a priest of the city of Jerusalem, he recognized the priest as one who already truly knew God. The condition of other Old Testament persons who were acceptable to God also guides Pinnock to his view of "pagan saints," a term he received from Jean Daniélou. In the New Testament, Cornelius is the key figure in establishing the teaching of implicit-faith. To Pinnock, the account of Cornelius teaches that God was present and active in the religious affairs of Canaanite culture. Pinnock's conclusion is that, "God never leaves himself without witness among all peoples (Acts 14:17)" (1988:159-62; 1995: 108-109).

David Clark demonstrates that the implicit-faith view differs from relativism and pluralism in that it teaches the necessity of Christ's objective, saving work. It also, differs from basic inclusivism in that it does not claim that one who overtly rejects God is a non-believer. The principle of salvation through natural revelation applies only to those who have never heard of God. If they on hearing of Christ immediately proclaim that Jesus is the one they have been following and expecting all the time they may well have been implicit believers. If they do not, real faith has probably not taken root in their lives (1991:42).

The implicit-faith view is not actually a part of most inclusivist pronouncements. The view is, however, closely allied to inclusivism and definitely a part of wider-hope theory. Clark writes:

> The point [belief in implicit-faith concept] is, however, that some can potentially be saved, based on the atonement of Jesus Christ, thorough the information content of natural revelation. This view solves the dilemma by denying, not God's willingness to save all, but the necessity of gaining he informational content for salvation from special revelation (1991: 43).

Clearly, the concept of implicit-faith stands well within the views of wider-hope theory and the possibility of salvation through general revelation. Inclusivists recognize the superiority of special revelation over general revelation and that no person can be saved by his/her own effort. They also recognize human sinfulness. But, they teach, because of general revelation, persons have the possibility of salvation even if they have sinned and never heard the message of Christ (Sanders 1992:234-35). Inclusivists contend that people are lost, not because they never hear the gospel, but because they reject the Father. Why, they ask, can one learn enough from general revelation to be lost but not enough to be saved?

Many Inclusivists also use the concept of "the Faith Principle." By this phrase, Sanders understands that Hebrews 11 teaches that one cannot please God apart from faith. Faith, says Sanders, involves three factors, truth, trust, and effective action. Genuine faith contains some truth about God, whether that truth comes from the Bible or God's work in creation. Faith, however, also involves a trusting response to God. If a person truly responds to God he/she will seem to live out their lives in a way approved of God (1995:36).

This concept of the Faith Principle guides Sanders and other Inclusivists to the idea that people are acceptable to God however limited their knowledge of God might be. "God," says Sanders, "judges people on the basis of the light they have and how they respond to that light." He continues by saying that he does not disagree on the need for knowledge. He does, however, question the degree of knowledge necessary for entering into a trusting (saving) relationship with God. He concludes saying,

> The central problem of salvation is not knowledge of God but faith in God. Having a right attitude toward God is much more important than doctrinal information (1995:38).

The conclusion is that the unevangelized may be reconciled to God on the basis of the work of Christ even though they are ignorant of Jesus. Sanders considers such persons as "believers" in God while those who know about Jesus are classified as "Christians." He sees continuity between believers and Christians (1995:38).

Inclusivists say the exclusivist's position that salvation comes only through explicit faith in the message of Christ does not provide genuine, universally-accessible salvation (1988:245). Most inclusivists would agree with Dale Moody's statement that God would not give a person enough light in general revelation to damn him/her but not enough to save him/her (1981:59). Such convictions lead inclusivists to affirm salvation in general revelation.

Inclusivism believes in salvation by works. The possibility of salvation being earned by works is not central to inclusivist thinking but is certainly evident. Pinnock even mentions what he calls the "ethical criterion for salvation." By this Pinnock means that a person who lacks New Testament faith but produces good works may be saved on the basis of the good works (1991:98). He suggests that even the atheist though rejecting his understanding of God, responds positively to him implicitly by acts of love toward his neighbor (Ibid). Sanders affirms Pinnock's understanding of the sheep and goats in Matt 25:31-40 as indicating that serving the poor is an adequate substitute for faith and may be one ground on which God saves the unevangelized (Sanders 1992:259). Nash rejects this entire line of thinking (1994:169-170).

Inclusivism believes in corporate election to service rather than individual election to salvation. Pinnock disagrees with his understanding of Augustinian theology and the teaching of "double election" *meaning that some are decreed to salvation and others to condemnation.* He calls this understanding "a tragic and influential error" (1992:24).

It is better to view God's love being for all and election to Abraham and his family a means to implement God's love to all humanity. Pinnock's conclusion is, "Election has nothing to do with the eternal salvation of individuals but refers instead to God's way of saving the nations" (Ibid, 24-25). The view of corporate election for service undergirds the inclusivists' view of universally-accessible salvation.

Inclusivism supports the concepts of postmortem salvation and conditional immortality. John Sanders contends for postmortem possibilities of salvation by attacking the passages usually employed to reject the idea. He declares that John 14:6 and Acts 4:12 teach that all who come to God through Christ will be saved but not that all who do not receive him will be lost. This interpreter uses these concepts to suggest another way of salvation for those who never hear the Gospel and for those handicapped (1988:247). Gabriel Fackre, an inclusivist who supports the view that every person will be given an opportunity to repent in a post death encounter, notes a variety of labels placed on the view—future probation, second probation, eschatological evangelism, postmortem evangelism, and PME. He prefers his term, "divine providence" to express the view that the unevangelized will be given an opportunity after death (1995:71-95). Inclusivists are understandably troubled by the thought of more being left in punishment than delivered from it. The answer to the problem, in Pinnock's mind, is either the "pagan saint" or "postmortem evangelism." Pinnock bases his hope of postmortem encounter on 1 Pet 3:19-20 and 4:6, which he thinks speak of an after death encounter with Christ at which the unbeliever will have a chance to repent. Should these reject Christ in the postmortem encounter, they would be lost but by their own choice rather than God's condemnation (1992: 149-56 and 168-89). Postmortem evangelism allows inclusvists to project hope for the unevangelized, for babies, and the mentally incompetent.

Readers should understand the difference in the belief on postmortem evangelism among Universalists and Inclusivists. *Inclusivists believe that one might still reject the offer of God*. Universalists believe that eventually all will come to faith. This important distinction should be maintained and understood.

Inclusivists say postmortem evangelism and annihilationism are both more biblically and theologically correct than the traditional view of everlasting punishment. These doctrines avoid the error of postulating infinite punishment for finite sin (Pinnock and Brow 1994:92-93). Pinnock declares everlasting torment to be morally intolerable. It makes God, says Pinnock, "a bloodthirsty monster who maintains an everlasting Auschwitz for victims whom he does not even allow to die" (1990: 251). John Wenham contends that teachings of everlasting punishment are neither loving nor just and in opposition to such teachings as God loveliness and glory (1992: 185-187). Michael Green asks what kind of God would rejoice in Heaven with the saved while below lost souls cry out in agony? (1990: 72). Stephen Travis calls the teachings of eternal punishment "vindictive" and "incompatible with the love of God in Christ (1980:135). Clearly, inclusivists maintain a view that rejects any eternal separation in the sufferings of Hell.

Inclusivists maintain that postmorten evangelism and

conditional immortality do not diminish the urgency for world missions. They see the uncertainty of the teachings of post-mortem evangelism and the loss of those who would miss the blessings of salvation during life to motivate for missions (Pinnock 1991:114; Fackre 1995: 94). Inclusivists believe that postmortem evangelism provides hope for adherents of other faiths, those who never hear the gospel, and to those who reject the Word (Pinnock and Brow 1994:94). Sanders declares that the time for a final decision about the gospel is the "day of the Lord" and not the day one one's death (1988: 251).

Inclusivism tends toward the concept of the "Openness of God." This view understands that God relates to the world in dynamic rather than static terms. God influences people but is also influenced by them. God only knows events as they happen. Human decisions and actions contribute to events (Pinnock, Rice, Sanders, Hasker, and Basinger 1994:16-17).

Inclusivists use this concept to further undergird their view that salvation is determined by one's response to light rather than a predetermined matter. Humans are free to accept or reject God's offer (Ibid, 174-76). Their belief in the "Openness of God" and salvation as a response to light contributes to the inclusivists' conviction of the possibility of salvation in world religions.

An Evaluation of Inclusivism

Inclusivists express dismay that evangelicals who accept the truth of Scripture do not support inclusivism and the belief in "pagan saints." Pinnock says that biblical teachings prove (and he contends that "prove" is not too strong a word) that God is prepared to be the God of pagan people (1992:27).

Evangelicals respond by pointing out that they do not accept many of the interpretations of the inclusivists. While praising the inclusivists' concern for the unevangelized, their use of Scripture, and their concern for adherents of other religions, most evangelicals cannot accept numerous basic teachings of inclusivism.

Most Evangelicals do not accept the belief that salva-

tion is available in non-Christian religions. In attempting to show that that one does not have to know or experience Christ personally to receive the benefit of his work, Inclusivists often misuse biblical passages. They underline 2 Pet 3:9 as saying that God is "not wanting anyone to perish" but fail to consult the remainder of the verse, "but every one to come to repentance."

Inclusivists tend to point to verses such as Rom 10:18 to teach that the revelation of God has gone out to all the earth. They often fail to show that in the context of the passage, Paul has declared that "everyone who calls on the Name of the Lord will be saved."

This conviction shared by most Inclusivists would actually diminish the importance of The Commission as it would mean that the non-Christian religions might bring more people to Christ than the witnessing church (Ott, Strauss, Tennent 2010:304). Exclusivists hold the position that a personal experience with Christ during one's lifetime is the lone path to eternal life.

Most Evangelicals believe that general revelation, while important, does not provide salvation. The basic belief of Evangelical Christianity stresses that God does desire the salvation of all but that to experience this salvation, one must know Christ. It follows from this view that to know Christ one must come into contact with him, generally through the message of the Bible.

Evangelicals also believe that God is sufficiently powerful to see to it that people come into contact with special revelation but admit that all persons in history have not experienced this contact with special revelation (see Clark 1991:35-36). Evangelicals do not see general revelation as providing a possibility for salvation but rather a gracious disclosure on God's part of his existence, perfections, and moral demands (see Demarest (1982:248).

Ronald Nash slices to the center of this teaching, saying that Romans 1-3 indicates that God has made important information available to all humans, through general revelation and that this revelation has failed to bring about salvation. Nash points to Rom 3:10 and 23 as support for his position (1995:111). He summarizes saying:

> Romans 1-3 seems clearly to contradict the inclusiv-
> ist's belief that people in non-Christian religions may
> be saved by responding in faith to the content of gen-
> eral revelation. Paul makes it plain that general revela-
> tion does not and cannot save (ibid)

Nash concludes saying that nowhere in Romans does Paul teach that general revelation is an instrument of salvation (Ibid).

In like manner, Nash refers to Inclusivist biblical inter-pretations of other passages. He shows in each case how passages such as Act 10 (the account of the Roman Cor-nelius), Acts 4:12, Roman 10:9-10, and John 14:6 each are more adequately understood from the exclusivist position than from the inclusivist. He shows the inadequacy of the inclusivist interpretations. Nash suggests that other passag-es such as 1 John 5:12, John 1:12, 20:30-31, 3:18, and 1 John 2:23 strongly support the restrictivist position (1995 127-28). Nash's final stand is expressed without apology as he writes: "The inclusivist support from Scripture stands on shaky ground and reflects a disturbing tendency to explain away clear biblical statements that run contrary to their po-sition" (Ibid. 128).

The teachings of some Evangelical writers seem to open the door, ever so slightly, to the possibility of salvation through general revelation. Sir Norman Anderson writes in such a way as to lead some to hear him affirming salvation through general revelation. He writes, "But might it not be true of the follower of some other religion that the God of all mercy had worked in his head by his Spirit, bringing him in some measure to realize his sin and need for forgiveness, and enabling him, in his twilight as it were, to throw himself on God's mercy" (1984:148-49). J. I. Packer answers that the answer to Anderson's question might be yes (1986:25). An accurate reading of Norman Anderson, however, hears him affirming the view of Stephen Neill to the effect that for the human sickness there is but one specific remedy, and this remedy is the Christian exclusive claim (Neill 1961:16; Anderson 1984:140 and 143).

One must, however, follow Packer's teaching. While ad-mitting that God is capable of providing salvation to some in general revelation and through the religions, Packer suggests it would be accomplished as among the Old Testament persons. Packer says that if some are saved through means other than special revelation, they will learn in heaven that they were saved by Christ's death and their hearts were renewed by the Holy Spirit. Readers should, further, hear the pronouncement of Packer who writes:

> We have no warrant to *expect* that God will act thus in any single case where the gospel is not known or understood. Therefore our missionary obligation is not one whit diminished by out entertaining this possibility. Nor will this idea make the anti-Christian thrust and consequent spiritual danger of non-Christian religions seem to us any less than it did before (Ibid).

Packer concludes saying that we need not spend much time mulling over the questions of salvation through general revelation or in the religions. We can leave those questions to God. We should be concerned of what we know as the universal need of forgiveness and the new birth and the invitation of "whosoever will." We should, according to Packer, "redouble our efforts to make known the Christ who saves to the uttermost all who come to God by him" (Ibid).

Some inclusivists seek support from the teachings of Millard Erickson based on his article, "Hope for those who haven't heard? Yes, but . . . ." (1975:122). Some readers perceive a leaning toward salvation in general revelation in the preceding article. Erickson, however, makes his position absolutely clear in his article, "The State of the Unevangelized and its Missionary Implications" (1998: 148-165). In this writing, Erikson makes clear that he rejects the ideas of implicit faith, postmortem salvation, and annihilationism. He concludes:

> In light of the foregoing considerations, we conclude that Christ's command to be witnesses to him throughout the entire world and to make disciples of all people is incumbent upon the church today. The mandate to mission should be accepted uncompromised by those who follow scriptural teachings. Theologies of "wider hope," universal accessible Salvation," and "salvation through general revelation," while engaging, are not biblically acceptable. The church remains obliged to respond positively to the mandate to "make disciples of all nations" (Matt 28:19) (1998:165).

Alister McGrath projects an interesting alternative within Particularist thinking. McGrath is convinced that human failure to evangelize cannot and should not be transposed into God's failure to save. Salvation is not, he says a culturally conditioned or restricted human accomplishment. It is ". . . God's boundless sovereign gift to his people" (1995:178-79).

McGrath suggests that salvation might come apart from the direct verbal transmission of the gospel message. He says:

> Where the word is not or cannot be preached by human agents, God is not inhibited from bringing people to faith in him, even if that act of hope and trust may lack the fully orbed character of an informed Christian faith. The doctrine of prevenient grace has been severely neglected in our theology of mission, so that we have overlooked the simple yet glorious fact that God has gone ahead of us, preparing the way for those who follow. In the harshly intolerant cultural climate of many Islamic nations, in which the open preaching of the gospel is impossible and conversion to Christianity punishable by imprisonment or death, many Muslims become Christians through dreams and visions in which they are addressed by the risen Christ. Perhaps we need to be more sensitive to the ways in which God is at work and realize the, important though our preaching may be, in the end God does not depend on it (1995;179).

Clearly, McGrath does not teach salvation through general revelation. He simply expands the boundary of special revelation to include direct relationship through the Risen Christ. His view does, however, deserve close attention as a possible answer to the questions surrounding the state of the unevangelized.

Evangelicals as a rule do not accept the possibilities of salvation through general revelation. Theologically they maintain the belief in the necessity of special revelation and the proclamation of the Message of Christ. They continue to state their belief that Christ is the only Savior and that the message concerning Christ is one ingredient in coming to salvation in him. The position on general revelation remains one of the large differences between Exclusivism and Inclusivism.

Only Jesus

Most Evangelicals would reject the possibility of salvation through God's Middle Knowledge. Little philosophical or theological support can be rallied for the idea. Sanders correctly evaluates Goodman and Lake somewhat negatively on the idea of salvation with no act of faith (1992:174). He is almost certainly correct is saying that Craig is more like an Exclusivist attempting to relieve God of blame for not giving all humans an opportunity to hear of Christ's salvation (1992:174).

The exclusive position finds deep concerns with the concept of God's Middle Knowledge. Jer 3:6-10 seems to teach that God had thought that Israel (the Northern Kingdom) would repent due to all the light God had given them. This did not happen and led to the destruction of this Kingdom. The few passages that seem to support the concept of "Middle Knowledge" (1 Sam 23:6-13; Matt 11:20-24) are simply not adequate to support the doctrine. The idea of God's Middle Knowledge does not answer the questions surrounding the lost condition of humanity and the state of the unevangelized.

Most Evangelicals believe that opportunities for repentance and faith in Christ are available only during one's lifetime. Ideas of postmortem encounter are not biblical teachings. Evangelicals understand that basing the doctrine of postmortem repentance on 1 Pet 3:19-20 and 4:6, places too much credibility on these most difficult verses. Some of the aspects of the doctrine inclusivists call the "Openness of God" go beyond scriptural endorsements.

Exclusivists point to numerous scriptural evidences that the opportunity for repentance is limited to one's lifetime. In the parable of the beggar and the rich man, no idea of the rich person having another chance surfaces (Luke 16; 19-31). The picture that Jesus gives of the separation of believers and unbelievers (sheep and goats) speaks of unchangeable separation (Matt 25: 31- 46). The parable of the wise and foolish wedding attendants seems to warn of the importance of decision (Matt 25:1-13). The Book of Hebrews warns that all people will face death and the judgment and that both death and judgment are eternal (9:27; 10:27).

Conclusion

Evangelicals agree with Pinnock that the views of inclusivists are uncertain and that direct evangelism is, therefore, the wiser course. Evangelicals think that many of the inclusivists' interpretations fall in this same trap, even if to a lesser state.

Evangelicals do not reject inclusivist intentions, emotions, or concerns. They simply reject many inclusivist interpretations. Evangelical understandings of biblical teachings drive them to maintain the conviction that salvation comes only through explicit faith in the one Savior, Jesus Christ (Nash 1994:11). Inclusivist viewpoints simply do not match with biblical teachings. Since the Bible is the ground for all Christian belief and practice, Exclusivists cannot accept the teachings and emphases of Inclusivism. We turn now to a systematic study of the Particularist approach to a Theology of Religions.

Only Jesus

CHAPTER 5

EXCLUSIVIST APPROACHES

The more biblically based theologies of religion are usually grouped together in categories called exclusivist, particularist, or restrictivist. This position contends that salvation is received only through an explicit act of repentance and faith directed to the historic, Living Christ during the believer's life time in response to the revealed message of the gospel (see Ott, Strauss, Tennent 2010:294). As mentioned previously, Paul F. Knitter, in his newer categories of theologies of religions, suggests the term "Replacement Model" for this view and divides the model into "total replacement" and "partial replacement" (2002:1-50).

Statements of Exclusivism

Dennis Okholm and Timothy Phillips correctly point out that the term Exclusivist has become so prejudicial that it precludes true dialogue (1995:16). The background of this statement is the clear fact that exclusivism in many minds is associated with arrogance, intolerance, dogmatism, and close-mindedness (see Toynbee 1957:164-65). This misconception is a widely repeated complaint and is lamented by Francis Clooney who writes:

> Exclusivists are generally presented unsympathetically, as fiercely ruling out the truth of other religions, proclaiming (sometime arrogantly) Christian superiority, having naïve views on world history, etc. But this is of course caricature; it is unfortunate that the exclusivist position is not presented in the best possible light (1989; 200).

The discussion leads Okholm and Phillips to join other writers and suggest the term particularism as a replacement for either exclusivist or restrictivist (1995:16). Understanding the view of Okholm and Phillips on the terminology and the inadequacy of restrictivism or exclusivism, this author would agree that the term particularism is preferable. To continue in conversation with the field, however, the previously used terms cannot be totally set aside. We will use the three terms interchangeably.

Ronald Nash forcefully expressed particularism's conclusion saying,

> Evangelicals believe that Jesus is the only Savior. There is no other Savior and no other religion that we believe that can bring human beings to the saving grace of God (1995:107).

Particularism, thus, answers the question, "Is Jesus the only Savior?" with an unmixed and uncompromising, "yes." Harold A. Netland declares that the central claims of Christianity are true and rejects answers from other religions that conflict. Salvation, says Netland, is simply not found in other religions (1991:9; 2004:42).

Exclusivists do not believe the Bible promises a second chance after death, salvation through general revelation, redemption through other religions, "anonymous Christians" or "Pagan saints," or other means whereby humans can earn God's salvation. Millard Erickson summarizes exclusivist thinking, saying, "Theologies of 'wider hope,' 'universal accessible salvation,' and 'salvation through general revelation,' while engaging, are not biblically acceptable" (1998:165). Roger Nicole sees no reason for Christ's coming if salvation is accessible in any other way (1979:3). Exclusivists reach these convictions by both biblical and theological paths.

Timothy Tennent proclaims that any statement of exclusivism must include three nonnegotiable truths. These basic teachings are:

- The unique authority of Jesus Christ, the apex of revelation and the norm by which all other beliefs must be critiqued (John 14:6; Acts 4:12; 1 John 5:11-12)

- The Christian faith centers around the proclamation of the historical death and resurrection of Jesus Christ as the decisive event in human history (Acts 2:31-32; 2 Cor 5:19; Col 1:20

- Salvation comes through repentance and faith in Christ's work on the cross and that no one can be saved without an explicit act of repentance and faith based on the knowledge of Christ (John 3:16-18, 36; 14:6) (2002:16-17).

I would add to Tennent's non-negotiable list a final statement to the effect that this repentance and faith would come *during the person's lifetime* (Luke 16:19-31).

The Southern Baptist Convention adopted Timothy George's positive and clear statement in a resolution in 1993. In this statement, the Convention declared as false teaching the view that Christ is evident in world religions, in human consciousness, and in the natural processes to the extent that one can encounter him and find salvation without any direct means of the gospel (1993:94). The statement continued saying that adherents of the nonchristian religions can receive salvation only though faith in Jesus Christ, the only Savior (Ibid). Fewer clearer statements of particularism exist.

This book accepts and promotes the teaching that salvation comes to one only through a personal experience with the historic and risen Jesus Christ during lifetime. Scripture teaches nothing different from or in addition to this truth. Particularism insists that Jesus is the one and only Savior. We can trust no other doctrine nor promise any extension to it.

The Biblical Basis for Exclusivism

Particularism bases its understandings squarely on biblical texts with full confidence in the authority, trustworthiness, and reliability of Scripture. The Particularist interpretation of Scripture rejects any ideas that Christ is one of several (or many) ways to God. The biblical position is that Jesus is the one, unique way to salvation. One authority states this truth in these words:

> When we speak about the uniqueness of Jesus Christ, we are not speaking about the uniqueness of the Christian religion, though a case might also be made for that. . . . even Christianity as a religious system must be judged by its faithfulness to biblical revelation, especially revelation about the person of Jesus

Only Jesus

Christ. Rather than speaking of the superiority of any religious system, we are talking about the uniqueness of the person of Jesus Christ as the one way to God (Ott, Strauss, Tennent 2010: 318).

Exclusivists point out that the New Testament world was a world of intense pluralism. Various religions and sectarian groups vied for the attention and dedication of the people. In this pluralistic setting, the early Christians centered on the Old Testament theme that YHWH alone was God and he alone should be worshiped. These early Christians also taught that Jesus Christ was the exact person of the one true God and worthy of all worship. These beliefs were included in the early Christians' assertion that Jesus is the one and only way to God (Ibid. 318-21).

Some texts, say exclusivists, affirm the unique place of Christ in salvation. For example, Acts 4:12 states and means that no person can come to God except through an explicit knowledge and experience of the Person and work of Christ. R. Douglas Geivett and W. Gary Phillips declare,

> We conclude the 'name' refers to the focus of God's universal redemptive plan in the person and work of Jesus Christ, who must be the object of explicit faith by those who want to be saved (1995:232).

Exclusivists find this same teaching in John 3:16-18, 36; 14:6; and 1 John 5:11-12 (Nicole 1979:3). Speaking directly of John 14:6, Millard Erickson denies that the verse is only metaphorical. Ronald Nash contends that it is hard to find a meaning other than a restrictivist interpretation in this verse (1996: 19; 1995: 127).

Exclusivists believe that the Apostle Paul points to human sinfulness and hopelessness in Romans. Jew and Gentile alike, who have turned away from general revelation and conscience, are, therefore, guilty before God (Rom 1:20, 2:15; 3:9). Some exclusivists teach that while the Gentiles could have come to God through general revelation, none have actually done so, nor will they. Apart from Christ there is only ignorance and hardness of heart (Rom 4:18) (Sproul 1986:53-54).

In Ephesians, Paul uses the harshest words to describe

those who are apart from Christ saying they are "without God" and "without hope in the world" (2:12). Restrictivists understand such texts as indicating that without special revelation of the gospel there is only sin and no salvation (Netland 1978:77-78). Exclusivists base this teaching on texts which teach the imperative of hearing, repenting, and responding to the gospel. These words call sinners to repentance and command believers to take the Message to all (Mark 1:14-15; 16:15-16; John 3:36; 1 John 2:23). The only proper object of faith is the "Name" which must be Jesus (Geivett and Phillips 1995: 235).

Romans 9 and 10 reinforce the exclusivist conviction that salvation comes only through explicit faith in Christ. Paul's words include the teachings that human instruments are a necessity for proclaiming the Message (Rom 10:13-21), that justification comes only through confession of sin and faith in Christ (Rom 10:9-10), and that his prayer for his fellow Jews is that they be saved (Rom 9:1-7). Hearing the gospel and turning to God through Christ are natural prerequisites for salvation. No one has been more religious than the Jewish people of New Testament times. Still, Paul understood they needed to be saved (Smith 1998:427).

Particularists, disagreeing with most inclusivists, interpret passages in Acts in ways that bolster restrictivism. The salvation of Cornelius (Acts 10:1-48) teaches, according to exclusivism, that this good and seeking Gentile needed the Message from Peter before he found salvation. Nash contends, "None of the inclusivist claims for this chapter stand up when we view Acts 10 in the proper light" (1995: 122). The account of the salvation of Cornelius is best summed up by saying "The story of Cornelius suggests that whenever the spirit of God prompts a response to God's revelation, God will faithfully provide explicit revelation about the saving work of Christ" (Ott, Strauss, Tennent 2010:336).

Further, Paul's own experience (Acts 26:4, 5) demonstrates that the devout and zealous Pharisee, Saul, did not enter a saving relationship with Jesus until he trusted in the Risen Lord. Nash concludes, "Even though Saul satisfied every requirement of inclusivist salvation, he was still a lost sinner (1 Tim 1:15)" (1995: 139). Paul's commission was to take the light to those in darkness not to those who could see (Acts 26:18) (Nash 1994: 174-75). Exclusivists are con-

Only Jesus

vinced that Paul confirmed that the philosophers in Athens were seeking but not finding the true God (Acts 17:16-34) (see Geivett and Philips 1995: 133-34, 222). The Book of Acts confirms the exclusivist view of salvation and the necessity of special revelation.

Texts that speak of the narrow way and the few that find it (Matt. 7:13-14; Luke 13:23-24; Matt 22:14) lead exclusivists to with sorrow, regret, and in contrast to their desires, recognize the biblical teachings that while a large number will be saved, these will be a minority when compared to unbelievers (Erickson 1996: 201-215). B. B. Warfield objected to the interpretation that more would be lost than saved (1952: 334-50). Charles Hodge, in agreement with Warfield, believed that more would be saved than lost (Hodge 1940: 3:879-80). Most exclusivists would agree that this question bvest be left in the hands of God.

Biblical teachings on eternal punishment lead many exclusivists to accept the view that only those who come to God through an explicit faith in Christ can be viewed as saved. Exclusivists deny the accuracy of the concepts of postmortem evangelism, Divine Providence, and annihilationism. They strongly question the use of 1 Pet. 3:18-22, 4:6 as providing any promise of postmortem hope for salvation (Garrett 1995:2:62-64). Nash contends that in these verses there is not the slightest hint of any postmortem chance at salvation (1995:131).

The same problems exist, according to exclusivism, with annihilationism. The Bible presents Hell and its punishment as eternal. The biblical teachings on Hell stand on the same logical and exegetical foundations as do the teachings on heaven (Grounds 1981:215). Timothy R. Phillips, objecting to the teachings of conditional immortality, declares that every alternative to Hell calls into question the person and work of Christ (1991:53). Concerning annihilationism, Millard Erickson says, ". . . we conclude that the theory of annihilationism in its various forms, as appealing as it may seem as a solution to some theological problems, cannot be sustained, philosophically, biblically, or theologically" (1996: 232).

Exclusivists think their position concerning a theology of religions rests on sound biblical interpretations and reflects the biblical viewpoint. Geivett and Phillips conclude:

> . . . Christian particularism seems to us to offer the best explanation of a wide range of facts about God and human existence. If there are unresolved difficulties for all three positions, and if the evidence is not "conclusive" in the strongest sense of the term, Christian particularism offers the most intellectually and spiritually satisfying account of the available evidence with a minimum of difficulty (1995:245).

We turn now to particularism's theological foundations.

Theological Foundations of Exclusivism

Exclusivism rests on a well-developed theological foundation. The viewpoint is not built on feelings of pride or superiority. Followers accept what they believe to be Scriptural and attempt to remain faithful to these teachings. Exclusivists take no pleasure in teachings of eternal separation. Exclusivism's theological foundations are:

Exclusivism holds to the necessity of special revelation for the salvation experience. This conviction, based on the exclusivists' belief in the authority of Scripture, considers special revelation and propositional revelation as imperative for salvation. The Word of God is instrumental in conveying God's truth and in guiding humans to salvation in the God who saves (Lewis and Travis 1991: 383).

In this view, exclusivists maintain that divine revelation constituted the only means whereby the true God has given genuine knowledge of himself and provided the only power to turn people from the worship of false gods. Speaking of Romans 10:17, Charles Hodge declared that "there is no faith, therefore, where the gospel is not heard; and where there is no faith, there is no salvation" (1940, 2:648). Exclusivism sees the proclamation of the gospel as essential for salvation.

Exclusivists hear the questions of Inclusivists regarding the condition of "Holy Pagans." Nash points out the error of equating the condition of the Old Testament persons who were outside the Jewish religion were in the same condition as persons outside of grace today. Pinnock declares that one who is informationally premessianic, whether living in ancient times or today, rests in exactly the same spiritual condition (1992:161). He further contends that Abraham's experience with Melchizedek and other persons praised as people of faith in the Old Testament shows that religious experience may be valid outside Judaism and Christianity (1992:94). In another writing, Pinnock declares that exclusivists fail to recognize genuine piety outside the Christian movement because they ignore the truth symbolized by Melchizsedek and that this mistaken theology ". . . creates in them a brittleness, rigidity, and narrowness in the presence of non-Christian people" (1988:159).

Nash disagrees with Pinnock's conclusions. He teaches that significant differences exist between the Old Testament followers of God and current unsaved peoples. Biblical teachings, says Nash, indicate that Old Testament and New Testament believers stand in a continuity as they share the covenantal relationship to God ". . . that is grounded on special revelation" (1994:127). Nash points to passages such as Rom 1:1-2:11; 11:11-24; Gal 3:8; 6:16; Phil 3:3 and Heb 9-10 to support his view (Ibid). Further, Nash points out that in the matter of Melchizedek, who is a priest of the Most High God, worshiped and served Yahweh as certainly as did Abram (1994:127-30).

Inclusivists tend to hold up the Roman Centurion, Cornelius, as an example of an outsider saved apart from special revelation (Acts 10). Inclusivists point to Acts 10:2 and mistakenly assume Cornelius was saved before Peter came. John Sanders declares exactly this concept (1992:254). The truth is that Cornelius was in the same spiritual condition as many Jews of his day who had not yet encountered Jesus (Nash 1994:138). Actually, the account of Cornelius indicates that God sent Peter with the message—a sending not necessary if Cornelius was already a believer (attention to this passage has been stated earlier).

The account of Cornelius can be taken to teach that when a person, whatever his/her status, location, or opportunity seriously seeks God, the Lord finds a way to provide the special revelation need for that person to trust him. The Bible, however, does not precisely nor directly teach this concept. God's willingness to search in ways beyond the ordinary could, however, explain Alexander McGrath's words concerning persons saved by visions of the Risen Lord.

In conclusion, Particularists believe that special revelation is necessary for salvation and leave the exact method of this revelation in the hands of the Living God. Bruce Demarest concludes that in spite of some positive features, natural man with only natural religion who lacks special revelation will have a fundamentally false understanding of spiritual truth (1982:259).

Exclusivism believes that general revelation does not provide access to salvation. Closely tied to the preceding truth, exclusivism holds with Harold Lindsell that general revelation is, "totally insufficient as a vehicle for salvation" (1949: 107). Exclusivism contends that while God does provide spiritual truth about himself and humanity through general revelation and in other religions, there is no redemptive truth in either because this knowledge of God is too fragmentary and distorted to guide to salvation (Demarest 1982:70, 259).

Exclusivists understand that no human lives up to the full light of general revelation which leaves the unrepentant sinner without excuse (Kraemer 1956; 340-48). Carl Henry adds that people are not lost because they do not hear the gospel but because they revolt against the light they have in general revelation (1949:40-42).

In his book, *Eternity in their Heart,* Don Richadson, points to "startling evidence" that non-Christian religions have great value and that this fact is often overlooked by evangelicals (1981: 89). Richardson contends that long before the various peoples of the world heard the gospel, God had prepared them for the Truth. His idea is that God has, through general revelation, paved the way for the acceptance of special revelation.

The accounts in Richardson's book excite the Christian heart. Tite Tiénou cautions against regarding too highly the place Richardson places on general revelation. Tiénou accurately describes the difference between general and special revelation, saying:

> While both general revelation and special revelation "speak" of Christ, the latter is much clearer. General revelation is like someone telling a lost traveler, "If you take this road you eventually will get to your destination." Special revelation, on the other hand, is like someone handing a clearly marked map to a lost traveler with the words, "If you follow this map you will get right to where you want to go (1991:214).

Richardson's view should not be taken beyond his contention that general revelation that is hidden in the religions makes it easier for them to accept redemption (1981:59). Tiénou helps us understand that general revelation may well make it easier for a people group to accept redemption but it does not make it possible for them to be redeemed (1991:214). Particularists deny the idea of salvation through general revelation alone.

Exclusivism builds solidly on the truth of the Triune nature of God. The Christian message is unintelligible apart from the doctrine of the Trinity. The teaching of the deity of Christ and the truth of God's triune nature is the hub from which all the doctrinal spokes of Christian proclamation radiate (Ott, Strauss, and Tennent 2010:314). The truth of the doctrine of the Trinity is that Christ is the apex of the revelation of God the Father. Christ is the standard from which all else is measured as Christ establishes the ultimate revelation of the Trinity (John 14:9). The truth of the Trinity and Christ demands that evangelical theology be both Trinitarian and Christocentric (Ibid.).

As the Second Person of the Godhead, Jesus Christ is the one and only possible Savior for humankind. Only this perfect Savior is able to draw all people to God (Heb 7:15). Only a sinless Savior can serve as the perfect, holy, innocent, undefiled, separate from sinners, high priest who can create right standing with God (Heb 7:26-27).

The profound difference between Christianity and the religions is the truth that Jesus Christ is divine. As Erwin Lutzer declares ". . . if there is but one God and Christ is the second Person of what we call the trinity, there cannot be other thrones that He must share" (2000:359). Lutzer continues saying, Christian faith is unique because it alone is centered in Christ, and Christ alone is God" (Ibid, 367). John C. Ellenberger's straightforward statement is,

> The message for today is the same as the invitation Jesus gave: "the kingdom of God is near. Repent and believe the good News" (Mark 1:15). The good news of the kingdom is that Jesus, and Jesus alone, has come to redeem the lost. People can find salvation only in Jesus, not in Buddhism or any other religion. (1991:227).

Trinitarian faith stands at the heart of Christian teaching and as the central aspect of Christian witness. Through trinitarian thinking we realize that God is on mission to redeem and bless all peoples. This divine quest is the *Missio Dei*, the mission of God. As Christians approach a theology of religions and discuss the place of the religions of humankind in relation to God's overall plan for his Kingdom, the discussion must always be in context of the *missio Dei* (Ott, Strauss, Tennent 2010: 315).

Exclusivism teaches that Jesus Christ is the one and only Savior for humankind. In contrast to many wide-hope theorists, Exclusivism holds that the Bible presents the God of the Old Testament as the one and only God and that Jesus Christ claimed himself to be both divine and savior, the only savior. Timothy George has succinctly written, "But throughout history, God has had one and only one plan of salvation for everybody everywhere—by grace alone, through faith alone, in Jesus Christ alone" (2000:21).

Carl F. H. Henry correctly points out that in the Old Testament, in the face of other *theos* and *elohim* the Bible presents the living God as the one and only Divine who perfectly and wholly fulfills the nature of El. God is the one and only God to whom the people must bow (Deut 7:9; 1 Kings 18:21; Deut 4:35; Exo 20:21ff) (2000: 21).

This one God claims not only exclusive validity among the Hebrews but also declares himself the only God of the Gentile world and in fact in the entire created universe (Isa 45:18-23) (Henry 1949:40-42). Henry states without equivocation that:

> The notion that God's historical covenants embrace all world religions as part of the church that finds fulfill-

ment in Christ, and that Christ is present in nonbiblical religious history from the beginning, is alien to biblical teaching and arbitrarily correlates religion in general with redemptive religion. The New Testament does indeed represent the whole cosmos and all history as finding its final reconciliation in Christ. But from this emphasis we cannot logically infer that nonbiblical religious writings point to Christ in some hidden way. While God's saving design in the Bible has certain universal implications, it does not welcome the world's works-religions as prefatory to the propitiatory work of the Redeemer. The nonbiblical religions and religious writing are not oriented to Christ (1983:363-64).

In The New Testament both Jesus and his followers included Jesus in the unique identity of the one true God who was the one and only way of salvation (Ott, Strauss, Tennent 2010:319). Jesus' claim to a unique identity was accepted by and continued in the teachings of his followers as seen in the following biblical truths:

- Jesus claimed to be the fulfillment of OT Promise (Matt 5:17);

- He claimed Universal Authority (Matt 24:35);

- He claimed the authority to forgive sin (Mark 2:5, 10);

- He affirmed his unique Relations to God (Matt 11:27; John 5:19-23);

- He received honor, reverence, worship reserved for God and took titles and references for God from OT (Matt. 14:33; 28:17; John 5:22-23; 20:28-29; Matt 21:16; Luke 20:18; Isa 8:13-15; John 10:11; Ezek 34:9-14; Psa 23:1-4); Jesus claimed to be the only way to God (John 14:6);

- His opponents understood these claims (Matt 26:65; John 5:17-18).

In his own teachings Jesus did not shrink from the declaration that he was God's anointed one, the Messiah. Christian teachings rest on the assurances of these pronouncements.

After his death and resurrection, Jesus' followers continued and extended the claims of deity and saviorhood that Jesus had made about himself. These claims were voiced in the fiercely monotheistic environment of first-century Judaism. The Christian community included Jesus in the identity or the one true God. They did not hesitate to give to Jesus Christ the devotion, titles, and worship that were reserved for God alone (Ott, Strauss, Tennent 2010:320). Their affirmation was proper for Jesus Christ who was and is God incarnate.

The disciples understood Jesus Christ as the unique identity, as deity, as God Incarnate. On this basis they presented him as the only Savior though whose life, death, and resurrection was and is the one and only way to God. God is one and desires to extend his love to all. For precisely this reason, the early Christians continued to share the message that Jesus Christ was the only way to God. The idea that peoples in all cultures and nations are genuinely seeking the one true God or that these people can find Christ in any religion or belief system is simply not expressed in the biblical revelation (see Stewart 2000:379).

While the New Testament books are in close agreement with the understanding of the uniqueness of Jesus Christ as the one and only savior, the truth is especially central in the Books of Colossians and Hebrews (Ott, Straus, Tennent 2010:321). The Christians in Colosse faced a syncretistic heresy that taught a vast pluralism. Paul directed these believers to act on the fact they had been rescued from the hostile spiritual powers or the "dominion of darkness (Col 1:13). The Apostle underscores the uniqueness of Christ as the one way to salvation. The Christians should have no other "gods" next to Christ (Col 2:9-15). Christ has defeated the powers of darkness and stripped away their ability to dominate believers (Col 2:16-21) (see Arnold 1996; 1997). Because of his unique power to save, believers should avoid any entanglement with the religious mixture that was prevalent in Colosse (Ott, Strauss, Tennent 2010:322-23).

The Book of Hebrews is at least as central in presenting Jesus Christ as the one and only Savior. To a group of Jewish believers, the author addresses a stern warning against returning to strictly Jewish teachings. Jesus Christ is superior to all other religious approaches and no ground exists for giving allegiance to any other religious system. "The only acceptable response to Jesus and his work is to steadfastly follow him and hold to him and his salvation (2:1; 3:12-14; 4:14; 6:9-12; 10:19-23, 35:36, 39; 12:1-2, 15; 13:11-15) (Ott, Strauss, Tennent 2010:323). Exclusivists are convinced that the Bible presents without compromise or turning the teaching that salvation rests in Jesus Christ and no other.

Exclusivism does not consider multiple paths to God. The concrete belief of Particularism is that Jesus Christ is the one and only way to God. Only in Christ will any find this way. Erwin W. Lutzer accurately notes that "The deity of Christ gouges a clean and unbridgeable chasm between Christianity and the other religions" (2000:359). Exclusivists reject both the idea that many paths lead up the mountain but all reach the top and that there are many mountains each of which have paths to the top.

Clearly then, particularism rejects the idea that salvation exists outside of Christianity. The religions of mankind do not contain the message of salvation by which people can come to the obedience of faith. As seen earlier, in Romans 9-10, the Apostle Paul prayed earnestly for the salvation of his countrymen, the Jews, that they might be saved. Certainly these Jewish people were religious. They even had the revelation of the Old Testament Scriptures and the meaning in the sacrificial system. Yet the Apostle declares that they are separate from God because they were attempting to establish their own righteousness rather than submitting to the right standing that comes from God.

If sincere participation in religion could bring salvation, these Jewish people would have had far more hope than others. With little effort we can find examples of notable people who have achieved great respect among humans because of their service (Gandhi, Confucius, Plato). Many of these respected persons remained outside the Christian faith and followed religions other than that of Christ Jesus.

The question often arises, Are these people saved? Romans 9-10 seems conclusive that *salvation does not rest in religion but only in Christ Jesus*. Ronald Nash points to Saul of Tarsus as an example that seems to solve this question. Nash points out that Saul or Tarsus, before his conversion, passed every test of the inclusivist requirements for salvation. He satisfied Pinnock's Faith Principle with plenty to spare and sought Yahweh's will in full diligence (Acts 2w:20). If, says Nash, inclusivism is true then Saul the Pharisee was saved. This conclusion was soundly by the converted Paul (Phil 3:7-11; Acts 9:1-19; 26:15-320.

Nash continues showing that Saul, while fulfilling every requirement the inclusivists mention for salvation among the unevangelized, was still a lost sinner (see 1 Tim 1:15-17). Continuing his discussion, Nash explains that if we begin with the premise "If A, then B" and then discover that B is false, we must conclude that A is also false. If the inclusiveist statement Saul of Tarsus was saved is false, we must also conclude that Inclusivism is false (1995:238-2389; 1994:174-75).

Christ Jesus is the one and only source of salvation; salvation is found in him alone; salvation is not available in the religions of mankind.

Exclusivism holds that faith in Christ and only faith in Christ makes salvation possible. This statement contains several truths—faith in Christ is the door to eternal life; faith in Christ alone is the door to eternal life, and this faith is a matter of grace rather than works. Inclusivists persist in declaring that an act of faith is necessary for salvation but equally insist that this faith need not have Jesus as its direct object.

John Sanders writes that people can receive the gift of salvation without knowing the giver or the precise nature of the gift (1992:224-25). He continues saying that saving faith does not necessitate knowledge of Christ in this life. He continues that God's grace is wider than the arena of special revelation and that God will accept into his kingdom those who repent and trust him even if they know nothing of Jesus Christ (1992:225). Pinnock adds that people are saved by faith not by the content of their theology (1992:157).

Exclusivists hold a certain amount of information is necessary to salvation and that awareness of this information is a necessary condition of salvation. This conviction finds its support in Rom 10:9-10. Exclusivists reject Sanders argument that while Rom 10:9-10 does teach that one who confesses Jesus as Lord will be saved it does not teach the reverse and say that one who does not confess Jesus is lost

(1992:67).

Sanders contends that Paul's statement should not be understood both ways. Such interpretation would be like, he says, to saying all Collies are dogs therefore all dogs are Collies. Thus, he teaches that saying all who receive Christ will be saved is not the same as saying all who do not receive Christ will be lost (1988:246-47).

Particularists maintain that faith in Christ is imperative for salvation and that salvation is not available to those who do not have faith in Christ. Faith in Christ to some degree requires some knowledge of the historic Christ, ie., special revelation (Erickson 1991:24). Nash sums up this matter as he writes:

> Inclusivists hold that faith can save people even though it is deficient in theological content, yet there is no place in Scripture that asserts this. Indeed Scripture teaches the precise opposite. While I agree that people are not saved simply by assenting to discrete information, I nevertheless maintain that saving faith has an awareness of such information as one of its necessary conditions (Rom 10:9-10) (1994:126)

Nash goes on to say that he thinks the preaching of the gospel must include specific information about the person and work of Christ and the truth that personal faith in him is necessary. It is reckless, dangerous and unbiblical, says Nash, to lead people to any idea that Jesus is not necessary for salvation (1994:126-27). Danger also resides in holding out hope or assurance that is not promised in Scripture.

Exclusivism holds firmly to the biblical teaching of salvation by grace. The biblical teaching of salvation by grace is central to Evangelical and exclusivist understanding. This teaching reveals that God's salvation is lovingly provided, freely given, and undeservedly granted (Eph 2:8-10). Grace is never earned, impossible to merit, and open to all. The doctrine of grace indicates that this loving provision originates with God (Rom 9:16), is inexhaustible in content, and beneficently made possible by the loving, divine sacrifice (See George 2000: 12-13).

Statements of wider-hope theories often reveal some tendencies toward a position of salvation by works. Ernest

Valea shows that while one Hindu teaching of liberation (*prapatti*) does tend toward the Christian meaning of grace, the primary emphasis in other religions tends toward some mixture of salvation by works (2011:6). Valea continues sowing the place of works even in Judaism and Islam as he writes:

> The monotheistic religions define salvation as entering a state of eternal communion with God, which means that personhood will not be abolished but perfected. However, they differ greatly on the way one can be saved and on the role Jesus Christ has in it. According to Judaism and Islam, salvation is attained by performing good deeds and following the moral law. According to Christianity this is not enough and the role of Jesus Christ as Savior is essential (2011:19).

Wider-hope teachings follow the works salvation approach and miss the deeper meanings of salvation by grace. No teaching is of greater significance to Evangelicals and Particularists than the truth of salvation by grace.

Exclusivism believes that the act of faith in Jesus Christ must come during lifetime. Exclusivists find no biblical grounds for postmortem evangelism, a "second chance," or "wider-hope" interpretations. As seen, they question reading postmortem evangelism into 1 Peter 3:18-4:6 as placing too much stress on a questionable and difficult passage (1996: 156). Millard Erickson declares that physical death marks the boundary of human opportunity (1994:150-57).

Exclusivism also points to a "proper" interpretation of Matt. 7:13-14 and 7:15-20 as evidences that what occurs during life determines what takes place after death. The account of the rich man and Lazarus cannot be relegated to simply a teaching of the correct use of material possessions. The story also suggests that physical death marks the end of human opportunity for salvation.

Restrictivists firmly believe that ". . . postmortem judgment is based on premortem conditions" (Nash 1995:134). Hebrews 9:27 settles this matter for most exclusivists as this verse established the order as death and then judgment. A person's status at judgment depends on the person's standing at death. After showing the plain teachings of Scripture passages contradicting ideas of postmortem salvation, Ronald Nash states:

> In all these passages and more, one a simple point stands out: Physical death marks the boundary of human opportunity for salvation. Anyone who wishes to argue that Jesus and the authors of the New Testament believed otherwise must shoulder the burden of proof. Given the serious implications of a belief in postmortem salvation, the total silence of Scripture regarding opportunities after death should trouble evangelical advocates (1995: 134-35).

Exclusivism holds no hope for postmortem salvation. While believers might feel some relief that those who reject God's message would have further opportunity, the promise is not to be found in Scripture.

Exclusivism understands that the lost select their own destinies and these destinies are eternal. Exclusivism teaches that the lost are not separated from God because they never heard the gospel. They are lost because they reject the Father, refuse the light they have, and turn away from the law written in their hearts (1986: 56).

Some exclusivists seek to soften the doctrine of lostness by suggesting a lesser degree of punishment, especially for those who never hear the gospel. Basing his view on Luke 10:12-14; 12:47-48, Loraine Boettner concludes that the unevangelized, while lost, will suffer relatively less punishment than those who have heard and rejected the message of Christ (1954: 120). This teaching is certainly within biblical parameters.

Particularists also interpret the Bible as presenting the duration of the separation of the lost from God as eternal. William G. T. Shedd characterized the teaching of an eternal punishment for sin as ". . . most severe and unwelcome of all the tenets of the Christian religion." He nevertheless provides his rational argument for just this eternal state (1886:161-62). Timothy Phillips contends that Jesus and the New Testament writers characterize hell as "a place of everlasting, irreversible, retributive punishment" (1991:53).

Writers such as William Fudge opt for the teachings of

what he calls Conditionalism rather than the view of Hell as an eternal punishment and separation. Fudge summaries his view saying:

> The fact is that the Bible does not teach the traditional view of final punishment. Scripture nowhere suggest that God is an eternal torturer. It never says the damned will writhe in ceaseless torment or that the glories of heaven will forever be blighted by the screams from hell. The idea of conscious everlasting torment was a grievous mistake, a horrible error, a gross slander against the heavenly Father, whose character we truly see in the life of Jesus of Nazareth (2000:20).

John Wenham, in concert with Fudge's view of Conditionalism, declares the teaching of unending torment to be sadism rather than justice as well as a viewpoint that negates the loveliness and glory of God. Wenham continues saying that the concept of endless torment is a hideous and unscriptural doctrine that has been a terrible burden on the message of the Church and a blot on the Church's witness (1992:187-88).

In his attempt to support the view of Conditionalism (Annihilationism) Fudge employs two untenable positions. First, he teaches that Jesus was annihilated on the cross (1994:143-145). Robert Peterson adequately points out that this view that Christ was annihilated on the cross conflicts with central biblical teachings. Such a concept would demand either the extinction of the human or the divine nature of Christ and both of these truths are clearly affirmed in Scripture. Peterson is correct in saying that the idea of Jesus being annihilated on the cross weakens rather than strengthens the case of annihilationism (Fudge & Peterson 2000:105-106; 174-78).

A second untenable position supported by Conditionalists relates to mistaken idea that God somehow takes pleasure in the suffering of persons who remain in endless torment according to the traditional view. The concept that Fudge tries to push off on Evangelicals is obviously a misunderstanding. Fudge writes:

> What we say concerning final punishment also reflects

on God's character. He is absolutely holy and perfectly just. On that, Scripture is too plain to be misunderstood. But are we to believe that God, who "so loved: the world that he gave his only Son to die for our sins (Jn 3:165, will also keep millions of sinners alive forever so he can torment them endlessly throughout all eternity? Is that the God we see revealed in the personal ministry of Jesus of Nazareth, who told his disciples that whoever has seen him has seen the Father (Fudge & Peterson 2000:81).

In the attempt to uphold Conditionalism, Fudge quotes Evangelist, Billy Graham, as questioning the literal teaching of fire in Hell. Graham's words, however, do not tend toward annihilationalism. Graham only says he is uncertain if the metaphor of fire is literal. But the Evangelist proclaims that the suffering in Hell is worse than burning—it is a thirst for God that "cannot be quenched" (1993:74).

Fudge goes so far as to charge that the belief in eternal suffering for the non-Christian brings actual pleasure to some traditionalists (Ibid. 208). Of course, this charge is baseless. Neither God nor his followers takes any pleasure in the destruction of the evil persons. The overwhelming passion of Exclusivists in relation to the lost is compassion and love. It is only with sincere regret and deep pain that Exclusivists accept the teachings of eternal, conscious punishment in Hell. Peterson correctly concludes that the view of Hell as eternal and state of those in Hell is conscious suffering is the "fit" with scriptural teachings on the intermediate state, the inseparability of the two natures in Christ, and the characteristics of final punishment (Fudge & Peterson 2000: 181).

John Newport declares this same view concerning the eternal nature of Hell. Newport writes:

> There are other tragic aspects of hell. There is the hopelessness of realizing that this separation is permanent, and that the condition of one's moral and spiritual self is similarly permanent. Whatever one is at the end of life will continue for all eternity (1989:314).

Exclusivism, therefore, rejects annihiliationism, universalism, and any other teachings that question the teaching of eternal separation from God. It is with greatest sorrow, regret, and distress that Christians hold this view, wishing it were otherwise. Faithfulness to the Word, however, allows no other way to understand God's revelation.

Exclusivism teaches that salvation is only reached through explicit, conscious faith in Jesus Christ and not through the non-Christian religions or cults. Mark Heim declares Christ as the sole and decisive mediator of the one salvation. He contends that forgiveness, reconciliation, and restoration to communion with God come only through the "narrow way" of faith in Christ (1985:138-39).

Hendrick Kraemer projects exclusivist thinking in his categories of "biblical realism" and "radical discontinuity." He sees a total break between Christianity and the religions (1938:69-73; 1962:120-25). Kraemer astutely questions the possibility of salvation in the non-Christian religions by asking how the Jews, the most prepared of all people, could have rejected Christ if the religions provided any way to God in Christ (1956:226-300).

Peter Beyerhaus, in the Frankfort Declaration, denies that Christ is anonymously present in the world religions and declares these religions are not vehicles of salvation without the direct message of the gospel (1971:115-180). Millard Erickson also denies saving power in the non-Christian religions and declares that adherents of these faiths, no matter how sincere, cannot be saved apart from explicit faith in Christ as revealed in the Christian gospel and through Christian witness (1993; 133).

John Piper shows that a massive change came with the Incarnation of Christ. The revelation of God in Christ demands a conscious and explicit faith for salvation to be possible. Piper sums up his view saying:

> Therefore, the gospel is not the revelation that the nations already belong to God. The gospel is the instrument for bringing the nations into this equal status of salvation. The mystery of Christ (drawing the nations into the inheritance of Abraham) is happening through the preaching of the gospel. Paul sees his own apostolic vocation as the means God is graciously using to declare the riches of the Messiah to the nations (Eph. 3:8) (2010: Kindle edition location 904).

Exclusivists obviously believe that salvation comes only by

an explicit act of faith in the historic Christ as communicated through special revelation. Salvation, therefore, does not reside in the religions.

Exclusivism sees a major difference in those who trust Christ and those who do not. Exclusivists do not find the concepts of "anonymous Christians," "pagan saints," or "implicit faith" in Scripture. The inclusivist idea that believing persons lived outside God's covenant with Israel and were therefore believers finds little acceptance among exclusivists (Nash 1995; 116-17; Clark 1991: 257-59).

The contrast between Christians and believers simply does not fit into the exclusivist understanding of biblical teachings. Exclusivism points to the teachings of Hendrick Kraemer and the concept of "radical discontinuity" as the proper view of believers and non-believers. A. R. Tippett refers to William Barclay's interpretation of John 14:6 which shows that the Master's statement meant that all other religions were at best broken lights, glimpses, fragmentary atoms of knowledge, and the only true and full revelation of God was in him, Jesus Christ (1964:32). In agreement with Barclay's interpretation, Tippett declares that Jesus's intent was to say that he was the true way, the living way, and also the only way. Tippett concludes, "If Jesus himself is true, the meaning of the statement is quite manifest" (1969:18). Tippett teaches that when Jesus claimed to be the only way he was speaking the truth. Such is the conviction of Exclusivism.

Exclusivists hold without apology that a vast difference exists between those who have the saving relationship with Christ and those who do not. Exclusivists accept the teaching of Matt 7:13-14 as speaking of a definite separation between believers and non-believers. They accept the Judgment teachings of Matt 25:32-46 as revealing an actual, future judgment at which time people will be eternally divided into two groups.

Exclusivism allows for the concept of continuity/discontinuity and points of contact between Christianity and those outside the Faith. Exclusivists recognize that through general revelation and the religions, some truth about God is available to humankind. This continuity between the religions and Christianity provides points of contact by which those who proclaim the message of Christ can contextualize the message for any culture. While this continuity certainly exists, the discontinuity equally exists—that is, the Bible promises no salvation in these religions or through the points of contact. The points of contact can aid in the communication of the gospel but cannot bring sinful humans into a saving relationship with Christ.

Missionaries must, however, be alert for these points of contact in order to more clearly proclaim the Message to people in the cultures of the world. The concept of points of contact is not the subject of this book, but a growing field of literature is available that includes Alan R. Tippett, *Solomon Island Christianity* (1967); *Verdict Theology in Missionary Theory* (1969); "The Meaning of Meaning," in *Christopaganism or Indigenous Christianity*, ed Tetasunao Yamamori and Charles R. Taber (1975); Don Richardson, *Peace Child* (1974); *Eternity in Their Hearts* (1981); "Redemptive Analogies," in *Perspectives on the World Christian Movement*, (1999); Marvin K. Mayers, *Christianity Confronts Culture* (1987); Peter Beyerhaus, "Possessio and Syncretism in Biblical Perspective," in *Christopaganism or Indigenous Christianity*; David J. Hesselgrave and Edward Rommen, *Contextualization: Meanings, Methods, and Models* (1989). These and other sources explain the concept and usefulness of the teachings of points of contact between Christianity and peoples who follow other religions.

Exclusivism realizes that the central teaching on the overcoming love of God does not cancel the equally central teachings on his holiness, wrath, and judgment on evil. Evangelicals view eternal punishment for sin and evil as neither an evidence of uncaring, any lack of power, nor an unloving spirit on God's part. As seen earlier Widerhope theorists, especially from the group who espouse annihilation, have declared that an eternal separation from God in Hell to be an unloving and therefore ungodly action (see Pinnock 1987: 40-41; 1990:243-60; 1992).

Exclusivists understand that God's love does not cancel out his holiness, wrath, and judgment on sin. Restrictivists, note that some place so much emphasis on the love and justice of God that they leave out, or at least limit, his holiness, justice, sovereignty, and his wrath upon sin. Christopher W. Morgan correctly writes: "So our understanding of God's love must be weighed against the whole fabric of Scripture, not just a small fraction of it (2004:214).

D. A. Carson teaches that the biblical teachings on the love of God cannot and should not be abstracted from the sovereignty of God, the holiness of God, the providence of God, or the personhood of God and other truths. The result of taking the love of God without proper consideration to his judgment and wrath against sin has led, says Carson, to the contemporary method of purging from the biblical message anything that culture finds uncomfortable. The final result is a theological error that overlooks a biblical certainty (2000:9-11).

Evangelicals accept and must maintain belief in the supreme love of God. At the same time, Particularists accept and act on the clear biblical teachings of God's justice, wrath against evil, and willingness to punish offenders. Attention has been drawn to John Frame's view that God's attributes exist in close relationship and connection to all the others. Frame uses the term "perspectival" in that each attribute describes something of the nature of God from a different perspective. The implication is that we must follow the teachings of these perspectives in our efforts to understand the nature and actions of God (2001:53-54).

Exclusivism recognizes the freedom of the sovereign God to work in ways unknown to Christians to save the lost of the world but are deeply aware that no such plan is revealed in Scripture. God can and does work in ways not comprehensible for human logic. Human logic and consideration never exhaust the truth of the Lord who created this world and all that is in it. God can work in ways not understood and not comprehended by man. If God has plans for the unevangelized, the infants, the handicapped, those plans remain in his hands. We will not refuse nor question his plan to save any. We also will not, however, trust any such plan of which God in his wisdom has not informed us.

Due to our lack of knowledge of any other way of salvation, however, exclusivists maintain the position that evangelism and missions must occupy the central place in Christian thinking. We can rely on no promise that the Eternal has not given. Nash helpfully advises:

> It is one thing for a theory to be false; harmless errors can sometimes be ignored. But errors that strongly dispose people toward actions that can compromise the church's mission on earth and place obstacles in the way of evangelism are too serious to ignore or excuse (1995:136).

We have no knowledge of salvation apart from an explicit, conscious response to the message of Jesus Christ. Christians would, therefore, be most unwise to rely on any concept of salvation outside of Christ, teach its possibility, or refrain from missions in the hope of it. The reader is reminded of E. A. Blum's admonition on the danger of teaching any concept that is not within God's promises (see pp. 51-52).

Exclusivisim upholds the biblical demands for Christian living and service but rejects any tendency to substitute good deeds for effective witness and missionary activity. Exclusivism recognizes that Christians have at times refrained from proper involvement in service to the world and its needs. They accept the biblical injunctions to seek justice and service to humankind and protect God's creation (Isa 1:10-26); Amos 5:24; Matt 2531-46).

While maintaining a firm conviction as to the necessity of social and ethical involvement, exclusivists avoid any trap of substituting service for witness. These two efforts must remain entwined. Belief in the particularist view should neither eliminate service or witness nor exalt one over the other. Biblical convictions keep in balance these two commissions from the Lord.

In summary, exclusivism maintains the view that Salvation resides only in Christ, accepted in response to his gospel during lifetime. As appealing as the wider-hope theories might be, exclusivists rest fully on the revealed teachings of Scripture. Apart from a Christian witness of this gospel there is neither promise nor assurance of hope for eternal life in the religions. With neither joy nor pride, exclusivists maintain the belief in the one Christ who can and will receive all who turn to him in faith.

Exclusivists equally believe that the experience of repentance and faith must take place during the lifetime of the person. Attention has been directed to Ronald Nash's proclamation that death is the boundary of human opportunity for salvation (1995:134) and John Newport's assertion that whatever one is at the end of life is what one will remain for eternity (1989:314). Nash also points to the writing of 2 Clement that, while not part of the New Testament, indicates the thinking of Christians in this early period. Nash quotes the early Christian leader, Clement, as saying, "after we have gone out of the world, no further power of confessing or repenting will there belong to us" (1995:132).

The conclusion of the Particularist view of salvation is captured by Michael Wittmer who in opposition to the idea of Rob Bell, writes:

> We are not saved by the universal fatherhood of God or by a cosmic Christ who has written the general principles of life in nature. We are saved by Jesus Christ, our Redeemer King, who in history's greatest and truest story defeated the powers of hell when he died for our sin and rose again. We are saved by Jesus, and him alone (2011:153).

The experience that opens the way for salvation come only in Christ Jesus and must come within the lifetime of the one saved.

Proponents of Exclusivism

All exclusivist positions are not exactly the same in regard to a theology of religions. As variation exists in the camp of the Universalists and Inclusivists, so variation is apparent within the Particularist persuasion. Careful readers will see a continuum of beliefs among these who basically agree that there is no salvation outside the Christian gospel. Okholm and Phillips declare that a "range of options within the general scheme" exists. They suggest one group, the hard restrictivism, as exampled by the writings of Harold Linsell. These writers see others within the particularist group whom they say take positions of pessimistic agnosticism toward the unevangelized and the optimistic agnosticism.

The first of these groups uphold that special revelation is necessary for salvation but leave the difficult question of the state of the unevangelized to God. The second group while not projecting a definite pattern for salvation apart from special revelation see some hope (1995:19-21).

This study suggests four groups of exclusivists--the Firm, the Uncertain, the Optimistic, and the Realistic. While respecting each of these groups, the author finds his most comfortable position in the grouping of Realistic Exclusivists. The four groups of Particularists is clearly presented the following diagram.

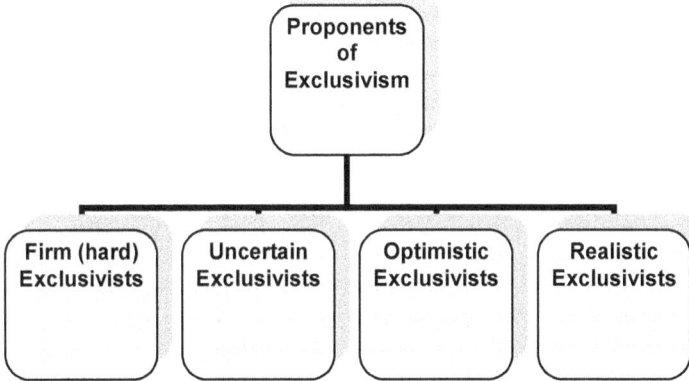

Firm Exclusivists

Firm exclusivists see such a radical difference in Christianity and other religions that they ascribe neither value nor truth the other faiths. Harold Lindsell, a leading proponent of this approach who is sometimes labeled a "hard" Particularist, not only sees no value in the religions but suggests they constitute evil (see Okholm and Phillips 1995: 19-20). God has not, even to a limited degree, revealed himself in the religions. Paul Knitter in his negative evaluation of particularism writes, "The theology of total replacement that we are considering looks upon other faith communities as so lacking, or so aberrant, that in the end Christianity must move and take their place" (2002:23).

Firm Particularist, Harold Lindsell takes the stance of opposition toward the religions. Christianity's contact with the religions and cults is, according to Lindsell, a "fight to the death" (1949:87-90). Lindsell believes that Scripture constitutes the only basis for finding salvation, that no salvation will be possible after death, and that general revelation has no saving power (1966:75). The only value he sees in studying the religions rests in increasing the ability to witness to their adherents and the only purpose of contact is that of pronouncing judgment and seeking their reconciliation with God (1945: 87).

Ronald Nash, while not so negative toward other religions as Lindsell, still reveals a firm exclusivist posture. He rejects the idea of salvation in general revelation, the concept of "pagan saints," and the possibilities of salvation apart from propositional revelation. He agrees with Harold Netland in criticizing the pluralists' failure to acknowledge the principle of non-contradiction (1994; 11-21; 54-55; 65-67; 75). Netland declares that the "price for rejecting the principle of non-contradiction is simply too high." He denies that the religions teach either the same doctrines or the same level of conduct as Christianity (1987:84-85; 1991; 36-37, 231-232). Netland's words express Nash's convictions perfectly.

Nash fears that in spite of the protestations that inclusivism does provide for missions that the view would work against carrying out the Great Commission (1995:134-36). No theological position that hinders the full involvement in the Great Commission is proper theology. The church is mission and must be mission and theology should enhance this mission. John Piper expresses his belief that the teaching that some can be saved apart from hearing the Gospel lessens the motivation for missions. In opposition to this viewpoint, Piper expresses his understanding saying:

> So I affirm again that the abandonment of the universal necessity of hearing the gospel for salvation does indeed diminish the urgency of world evangelization. And I say again that this is not the main reason for affirming the necessity of hearing and believing the gospel for salvation. The main reason is that the Bible teaches it, and therefore the good of man and the glory of God are most honored by it (2010: Kindle edition location 904).

Some firm exclusivists base their views on the theology of a limited atonement. If Jesus died only for those whom God in his election chose to redeem, then there is no question about any universally-accessible salvation. Loranine Boettner declares that persons who are providentially placed in areas of "paganism," such as western China, can no more accept

Jesus than they can accept some modern inventions they have never seen. When, says Boettner, God places people in conditions where the Word will not reach, it indicates that God does not intend to save them any more than he intends the continuously frozen soil of northern Siberia to produce crops. Had God intended otherwise (for people outside the hearing of the gospel and for the barren soils) he would have supplied the means for reaching such ends (1954:120). The author of this book finds little help from nor biblical support for this position.

Rigid exclusivists hold firmly to the biblical truth of the necessity of explicit faith in Christ and the necessity of proclamation of the gospel. They may exhibit a too rigid stance in their failure to see beauty or good in the religions. To acknowledge good and beauty in a body of teachings does not endorse these teachings. Further, rigid exclusivists tend to neglect finding any points of contact between the religions and Christianity. The deficiency in the rigid exclusivists rests more in their attitudes than in their doctrine. One would like to hear some larger statement of regret at the lost condition of people around the world.

The Uncertain Exclusivists

Some writers, who would deny themselves being pluralists or inclusivists, do not sound a certain note in regard to Jesus as the only savior and explicit faith in his gospel as the only way. Some might place Karl Barth, at least in his later writings, in the camp of uncertain exclusivists. While seeking to avoid universalism, Barth's concept of universally effective redemption affirmed that Christ did reconcile all persons to God through his death. All people, therefore, receive benefit from his death (1960:61).

In reaching this view, Barth takes seriously (and literally) texts such as Romans 5:18-19, 1 Corinthians 15:22, and 2 Corinthians 5:19. Barth also championed a view of election in which God has elected Christ, and, with him, all of humanity. Thus, Barth seems to say that all have been reconciled to God, but many may not be aware of it. These who are unaware of Christ's work will not be fully experiencing the benefits of this reconciling work (1960:61). Barth thus sounds a somewhat uncertain position concerning exclusivism.

Only Jesus

The Roman Catholic Jacques Dupuis also is a bit uncertain about Christianity and the religions. Dupuis denounces the relativistic Christology of the typical pluralist but also sees in some Hindu teachings elements of truth and grace that can complement Christian understandings. Christianity does not complete the religions, says Dupuis, but there is a mutual complementarity by which Christianity and the religions mutually enrich and even transform each other (1997: 305).

E. Luther Copeland, who acknowledges indebtedness to Dupuis, declares that Dupuis does not fit the pluralist mold. If a pluralist, says Copeland, Dupuis is a "borderline pluralist." Copeland likens Dupuis to other non-pluralists such as Gavin D'Costa, Kenneth Craig, and Norman Anderson, all of whom show some tendency to seeing possible saving light in the religions (1999: 32-39). These writers, while not pluralists, do not state clearly and definitely that Jesus is the only Savior and that explicit faith in his gospel is the one ground of salvation.

Copeland explains his own view in terms of a somewhat uncertain exclusivism. He clearly states his belief that divine revelation exists in the whole of human culture, including the non-Christian religions. He further declares that some, perhaps many, who never hear the Christian Gospel in this life will be saved whether or not they profess the beliefs of the Christian religion. Copeland adds that no one is saved apart from the redemptive work of God in Jesus Christ. Some may, he says hear and reject the gospel and still be saved because they reject it for valid ethical reasons (Ibid, 144).

These writers are not pluralists, although in some ways their views sound disturbingly like those of inclusivists or even Universalists. They are classified as "uncertain exclusivists" because they express less than a clear, straight forward conviction of salvation only through the gospel of Christ.

The Optimistic Exclusivists

Through Christian history, writers have suggested that while salvation is only in Christ (a definite Particularist statement) there remains a possibility that the Eternal God will intervene in some unknown way. We place writers who demonstrate this persuasion in a group, Optimistic Exclusivists. As seen earlier, Dennis L. Okholm and Timothy R. Philips call this approach "pessimistic agnosticism toward the condition of the unevangelized" (Okholm and Phillips 1996:20).

Other exclusivists, such as Lesslie Newbigin and Carl R. Braaten, while maintaining that Christ is the only Savior, still hold the hope that God will successfully extend salvation to much of humanity (Aldwinckle 1982: 215). Braaten conceives this extension as coming through an unspecified provision whereby "God is at work behind the backs of the plurality of world religions." This possibility exists, according to Braaten, because the religions "somehow speak of Christ" (1980: 5-7). Equally hopeful as Braaten, Newbigin also desires the salvation of non-Christians but contends it will not be through the religions (1969; 1989).

Both Braaten and Newbigin question the exclusion from salvation of all who do not respond to the explicit message of Christ. Braaten says this view opens a wide chasm between two irreconcilable halves of humanity—but God's half will be smaller than the Devil's. He says that the outlook of mainline exclusivism makes heaven a sparsely filled place with only a few "card-carrying" Christians (1980:7). Lewis and Travis resist this hopeful stance of Braaten and Newbigin saying, "Braaten believes in some kind of universal salvation; most evangelicals believe only in a universal Savior" (Lewis and Travis 1991: 399).

Some hopeful exclusivists find solace in the direction of annihilationism or conditional immortality. For instance, John Stott, who finds the concept of eternal conscious torment emotionally intolerable, expresses this hope. He reaches this view by taking the biblical pictures of the killing and destruction of the wicked as termination rather than perpetuation. Eternal punishment for finite sin, he says, violates the justice principle. Stott also thinks the eternal existence and suffering of the wicked contradicts texts that speak of God's final and complete victory over evil (Edwards and Stott 1988:312-29).

Some hopeful exclusivists opt, along with inclusivists, for the view of postmortem evangelism. George Lindbeck, for example, asserts that eternal punishment is not only psychologically and sociologically untenable but is "inhuman and un-Christian" (1973:281-89; 1984:46-71). Lindbeck is, however, unwilling to affirm that saving faith can be wholly anonymous. He thinks faith must be in some measure explicit—that is, *ex auditu* (from hearing).

This conviction leads Lindbeck to a near inclusive approach saying that since hearing is imperative for faith, then some will hear the Message after death (1984:57). Most exclusivists will, however, accept neither postmortem encounter nor annihilationism as ways out of the dilemma of eternal separation.

Another option for hopeful exclusivists is that of reflective agnosticism (Lewis and Travis 1991: 401). John Stott seems to fit into this category as he cherishes the hope that a majority of humans will be saved—although he does not know exactly how this will happen (Edwards and Stott 1988:327). Lorraine Boettner and Bruce Demarest both hold out some hope that God may have some way of dealing with the lost. While admitting that no direct biblical evidence holds out this hope, Boettner hopes that God through some "extraordinary method" will gather some of his "elect" from the unevangelized (1954: 119-20).

Demarest also hopes for some extraordinary means of special revelation, perhaps part of the "secret things: of Deuteronomy 29:29 that will result in salvation for the unevangelized. He insists, however, that none will be saved apart from hearing the message of Jesus (1982: 250-62). These hopeful exclusivists hold to the necessity of the message of Christ in the salvation process but hold a vague and undefined hope that God will find a way.

Alister E. McGrath has another hopeful suggestion to which attention has been directed earlier. He says that in places where the Word of God is not, or cannot be proclaimed by human agents, that "God is not inhibited from bringing people to faith in him, even if that act of hope and trust may lack the fully robed character of an informed Christian faith." Prevenient grace, Says McGrath, has been severally neglected in the theology of mission. Missionary theology has overlooked the glorious truth that God has gone before, preparing the way (1995: 179).

So what of those who never hear the message? McGrath

answers that it is a "flawed theology" that writes off the vast majority who ever lived and who were deprived of hearing by matters of geographical and historical contingency. This view limits God's modes of action, disclosure, and saving power and compromises the gospel's universality (Ibid, 178). According to McGrath, in the harshly intolerant cultural climate of many Islamic nations, where the open preaching of the gospel is impossible and conversion to Christianity punishable by death, many Muslims report they have come to Christ through dreams and visions in which they were addressed by the Risen Christ. McGrath's suggestion to the Christian movement is that Christians become more sensitive to the ways in which God is at work (Ibid 179). This position, certainly different from many exclusivists, falls clearly within the hopeful exclusivist group.

Hopeful exclusivists, realizing and accepting that they must maintain belief in Jesus as the only Savior, seek some way to deal with the frightening tragedy of lostness. Almost admitting an emotional bent to their thinking, hopeful exclusivists seek some ray of promise—especially for the unevangelized. Most exclusivists find these alternatives both unrealistic and unsatisfactory.

The Realistic Exclusivists

Realistic exclusivists answer the question, "Is Jesus the only Savior?" in a more direct and less emotional manner. They stand on their belief in the total authority and reliability of biblical revelation and find no genuine promise of salvation apart from an explicit faith in Jesus Christ. They do not, however, demonstrate any harsh or critical feelings toward followers of the religions.

Realistic exclusivists find in Scripture no promise of a second chance, postmortem evangelism, or salvation in the other religions. They hold to the teachings of the uniqueness of Jesus Christ, and the necessity of explicit response to the explicit gospel, the need for proclamation of the gospel, and the necessity of decision during lifetime.

Realistic exclusivists refuse to promise anything not directly proclaimed in Scripture. Their realistic stance finds its foundation in the acceptance of biblical teachings on salvation and lostness. They are, however, realistic enough to accept God's sovereignty to work outside their understanding and provide other ways. Their realism comes forward in the belief that we must live and serve in the light God has given and that revelation teaches that no salvation exists apart from the explicit response to the gospel.

Realistic exclusivists admit to some truth, beauty, and contribution to human culture in the religions. They also affirm that the religions and general revelation can provide points of contact between Christianity and the religions. These points of contact provide avenues for communication with the adherents of the religions but not a way to salvation without the Message of Christ. These aspects of realistic exclusivism divide it from rigid exclusivism.

A leading proponent of realistic exclusivism, Hendrik Kraemer, expressed his concepts of "biblical realism" and "radical discontinuity" (1962: 96-108). Harold Netland declares Kraemer the outstanding figure in the exclusivistic camp and Kraemer's *The Christian Message in a Non-Christian World*, the classic expression of Christian exclusivism (1991:180).

Kraemer sees no way of salvation other than Christ. In Christ, says Kraemer, God revealed not only his nature but also human nature. This revelation is, therefore, at the same time an act of divine salvation and an act of divine judgment. It is humanity's refusal to recognize and act on this grace that results in divine judgment (1938: 69-71). Biblical realism relates both to the revelation of God in Christ and the necessary response to this revelation.

"Radical discontinuity" expresses Kraemer's conviction that no common ground exists between Christianity and the other religions. Kraemer explains that this concept does not belittle nor make light of the religions but only emphasizes the newness and uniqueness of Jesus Christ, whose nature and works never arose within the hearts or teachings of humans. For Kraemer, conversion does not mean being converted to Christianity but to Jesus Christ (1962: 96).

Kraemer's concept of radical discontinuity does not mean there is nothing true or of value in the religions. Neither does Kraemer directly state that no point of contact exists between Christianity and the non-Christian religions. It does mean that the other religions even when they employ words such as grace or love, fail to actually deal with the great problem of human sin. The religions are in error because in essence their teachings consist of "self-deliverance." The great point in biblical realism that forms the basis of the radical discontinuity between Christianity and the religions is the Person of Christ (Ibid, 98-99).

The realistic exclusivism of Hendrick Kraemer allows no teaching other than a unique revelation and salvation only in Jesus Christ (1956: 375-76). Kraemer sees points of contact between Christianity and the religions and also calls for continuing dialogue. He insists, however, that in this dialogue, the Church maintains itself resolutely as the Church of Jesus Christ (Ibid, 375-77).

Kraemer thus sees salvation only in Christ and only through an explicit experience with Christ. In his response to William E. Hocking and the "Laymen's Foreign Mission Inquiry," Kramer affirmed in the strongest terms the missionary motivation he felt was compromised by the strongly pluralistic position advocate by Hocking and the Protestant Liberalism of his day (1938:292). He may represent exclusivism at its best.

R. Douglas Geivett and W. Gary Phillips contend that their conviction that Christianity is uniquely true and that explicit faith in Christ is necessary for salvation differentiates them from Inclusivists. They claim their view is better supported by both biblical and extrabiblical sources.

These writers ask about the stakes of holding any form of pluralism or inclusivism if the particularist view is correct. They correctly answer that if particularism is right, and they think it is, then pluralism and inclusivism both offer only a dangerously misleading assessment of the human predicament. Particularism is, they say, simply the best and most spiritually satisfying alternative to the question of the theology of religions (1995:243-45).

John P. Newport fits in the realistic exclusivists according to the description of James V. Hogue (Hogue and Smith 1989:186-87). Newport calls for "narrow mindedness" by which he means that while one is open to adjust his beliefs he is convinced these beliefs are not likely to change without being convinced both intellectually and intuitively.

Only Jesus

This writer does not see salvation in other religions but also calls for a conditional exclusivism that does not turn any faith system into idolatry (1978:175-77).

Newport declares that all non-Christian religions belong to one biblical category, sin. All religions, except Judaism remain equal distance from Christ. While one is either Christ's or not, Christians should approach adherents of other religions with "being" and "witness" (1989:412-13). Ott, Strauss, and Tennent mention Newport's position as a modern treatment of exclusivism (2010:295).

M. Thomas Starkes also provides a major contribution from his emphasis on dialogue with the religions. The dialogue should be servanthood based, personally open, non-attacking, continuing, and reflective of the image of God in the process. The purpose of dialogue is not winning a debate but sharing the gospel of Jesus Christ (1978:178-79). The emphasis on dialogue suggests a valid way of approaching adherents to other religions (see also, Starkes 1972 and 1981). Questions concerning the nature of proper dialogue are discussed in other sections of this book.

C. Gordon Olson falls seamlessly into the realistic exclusivist position calling Jesus Christ "the only light in the deadly night" (1998:65-80). Olson points to the statement by John Sanders that in effect says that Jesus could have settled any controversy over explicit faith being necessary for salvation with one statement (see 1992:19). Olson contends that as matter of fact Jesus provided exactly this statement in John 3:16. The clear teaching of the New Testament, according to Olson, is that the only way to escape perishing is by "present-age," explicit faith in Jesus Christ (1998:78).

James Leo Garrett, Jr. espouses the view of realistic exclusivist with a most helpful aspect. He teaches that Christian salvation comes only through personal faith in the incarnate, crucified, risen Christ (1990, 1995 1:106). Demonstrating his exclusivist convictions, Garrett says that there is no way for a Buddhist, a Hindu, or a Muslim to appropriate the saving grace of Jesus Christ while remaining in his own religion. Garrett's most helpful aspect is his emphasis that the church's proclamation should be exclusivist so as not to promise salvation outside the conscious acceptance of Jesus and the gospel. He goes on, however, to state that in God's sovereign freedom, he might effectually work outside the boundaries of exclusivism (1995:1:163).

In well-taken emphasis, Garrett is actually calling for humility on the part of those who follow the particularist position. The understanding we have through God's revelation tells us only of salvation through an explicit experience with the historic Christ through the actual hearing of God's Word. God is, however, sovereign. He can, if he wills, create another way of reaching people. Garrett is correct in saying that our proclamation must rest on the revelation we have. We should not, however, restrict God. Witness, dialogue, example, and prayer remain the best approaches for Christians in their relationships with adherents of other religions.

Garrett's final word on a theology of religions shows his faithfulness to the exclusivist position. Garrett says,

> The Christian claim is that revelation in Christ is ultimate, not to be superseded by Buddha or Krishna or Mohammed or Baha'allah (1817-92) or Joseph Smith (1805-44), or Mary Baker Eddy (1821-1910) or Sun Myung Moon (1920)" (1995:1:196).

Garrett's view is that the revealed position is the correct understanding. He, therefore, fits firmly in the pattern of realistic exclusivism.

Winfried Corduan also expresses convictions that place him in the camp of realistic exclusivists. Corduan takes issue with Pinnock's view that seems to say that a sincere seeker can experience God's grace and mercy even if entrapped within deficient beliefs (Pinnock 1990: 365; 1992:158). In disagreement with Pinnock, Corduan states his conclusions that religions even if they are derived from original theism contain elements that can be seen as preparatory for the gospel but also contain beliefs not taught in the Gospel. The Gospel of Christ cannot be, he says, merely the fulfillment of such religions (2000:141).

Corduan also refuses to see general revelation asable to save since the religions include beliefs inconsistent with biblical truth. Romans 1, says this writer, teaches a general awareness of God, but also teaches that humans will deny God and follow idols. He concludes, "I cannot think of one teaching of a major non-Christian religion that, given its own formulation rather than one imposed on it, is actually competent to open a person to the grace of God within its own framework" (2000:141-42). Corduan's conclusion is that the cross cannot be avoided with an objective examination of world religions and the cross does not find common ground with Sakyamuni, Amida, Shiva, or Muhammad (Ibid).

John Piper should also be considered a realistic particularist. His view is obviously that of Jesus Christ as the one and only savior. He calls for a conscious decision for Christ. He points to a definite and eternal separation between the Holy God and sinful humans. He is convinced that the teachings of wider-hope theories are detrimental to the motivation for world evangelism. Piper's clear statement is:

> Since the incarnation, God's will is to glorify his Son by making him the conscious focus of all saving faith. Without this faith—faith resting consciously in Jesus as he is presented in the gospel—there is now no salvation (2010:Kindle edition).

Piper extends this teaching saying:

> Paul and John are of one mind: people only come to saving faith through the word of the gospel of Christ. The sheep hear the voice of their Shepherd through the word of those who are sent (John 10:4, 14; 17:20); and Paul knows himself to be sent in this way: "I am sending you to open their eyes, so that they may turn from darkness to light and from the power of Satan to God, that they may receive forgiveness of sins" (Acts 26:17-18). Apart from the work of the Holy Spirit, who works through the word of the gospel of Christ (1 Peter 1:23-25), there is no faith and no new birth and no salvation. This is why "repentance and forgiveness of sins should be proclaimed in his name to all nations" (Luke 24:47) (2010:kindle edition).

Exclusivists believe in objective, biblical revelation, and in the basic doctrines of Christianity. They understand that the Bible clearly teaches the finality of Christ and his salvation. These convictions lead exclusivists to reject all forms of pluralism and inclusivism. The same commitments push evangelical Christians to maintain their commitment to exclusivist views of a theology of religions (McQuilkin 1994:50-51).

Evaluation of Exclusivism

Exclusivism or Particularism holds much more firmly to the basic teachings of evangelical theology than either pluralism or inclusivism. The rigid exclusivists probably have too little respect for the world religions. The hopeful exclusivists hold out desires for salvation that are not promised nor supported by biblical teachings. The uncertain exclusivists, in spite of their protestations otherwise, in many of their teachings sound much like inclusivists.

The realistic exclusivists most closely follow sound biblical interpretation and acceptable theology. Realistic exclusivists should remain solidly faithful to their biblical roots but also accept the freedom of the sovereign God to find the lost in some way he has not revealed in this age. Evangelicals cannot, however, trust in this hope.

As mentioned earlier (pages 48-49), E. A. Blum is correct in his statement that if any should accept and act on the concepts of any approach other than exclusivism and be wrong, the loss would be a disaster (1940: 61). We must seek to share Christ's message with all people for the promise that some will believe the message as that is the only certainty we have.

We must also remain faithful to the understanding that one who does not embrace God's salvation during that person's lifetime misses the tremendous blessing of living with and for Christ during this earthly walk. Salvation in Christ is more than eternity in Heaven, as great a promise as that is. God's salvation provides the daily experience of the Lord and the constant guidance of his Spirit.

The Bible promises God's salvation only to those who respond with an explicit decision to receive the historic Christ through repentance and faith during their lifetimes. Note these emphases in the preceding sentence. The statement emphasized that the condition of receiving the redemption of God and Salvation in Christ rests on the "explicit decision" of accepting Christ. By explicit decision we mean an actual personal relationship voluntarily and consciously entered by a seeking person.

This personal relationship is entered through the experience of repentance (turning away for sin and self-centerness) and turning to faith in Christ (faith). Repentance and faith are centered in the historical Christ who lived, died, was resurrected, taken back to Heaven, and will someday return to judge all humans. This experience of salvation must take place within the life-time of the person as the Bible promises no future (after death) opportunity.

The biblical promise is certain but also limited. Christ and his righteousness (right standing with God) is imputed only to those individuals who trust him for salvation. This central teaching is supported by Luke 24:47; John 1:12; 3:16-18, 14:6, 17:20; Acts 4:12; 26:15-18; Rom 5:1; 6:23; 10;1; 2 Cor 5;18-21; Eph 1:7; 2:8-10; Phil 2:5-11; Col 1:9-14; 1 Tim 2:4-5; Heb 1:2-4; 1 Pet 1:17-21. Evangelical Christians contend that we have no promise beyond the assurance that those who believe during their lifetimes will be saved.

If there is any other way to salvation, God's Word tells us nothing about it and makes no promise concerning it. Christians must act on the only light we have and proclaim the Message of Christ to all peoples. We cannot trust in any wider-hope no matter how attractive the idea might be or how much we might desire this possibility. No human logic nor approach that brings some promise can lead us to any assurance that hope exists for those not in relationship with Christ. *The Scriptures promise no other way.*

Christians must live strictly in the light of God's revelation, primarily in Scripture. We cannot legitimately add to or take from God's Word. We must refrain from promising anything, even hinting at anything which Scripture does not promise or support (Orr 1987:345-46; Demarest 1982:70, 354; D'Costa 1986;81). The wider-hope theories turn aside from biblical foundations to human assurances that lack any authority whatsoever.

Eternity for multitudes is too significant to chance the eternal salvation of these peoples on concepts not clearly taught in Scripture. Christians must remain strictly in line with God's revelation and leave the condition of the unevangelized in the hands of the all-knowing and all-loving Father. On the importance of remaining firm in our belief in the authority of Scripture, John Piper writes:

If we are cut loose from the anchor of God's Word, we will not be free. We will be slaves of personal passions and popular trends (2010: Kindle Edition, 940).

Christians should accept the biblical truths and recognize that there exists no promise or biblical assurance for salvation in religions or cults other than Christianity. This conviction does not keep Christians from recognizing beauty, dignity, and contribution in the non-Christian religions. The expressions of human belief (in religions and cults) are not evil—only wrong. None of the religions or cults brings sinful humans to God's salvation. None provides the intense joy of Christian living in the day-by-day experience. None offers the same promise to a broken world.

Christians should, with broken hearts, accept the lostness of humankind apart from Christ and his gospel. Our great desire to have all humans follow our Lord must not drive us to a sentimental acceptance and expression of unbiblical ways of salvation. A realistic assessment of biblical teachings concerning lostness drives us to share the Good News with all peoples. Belief in eternal separation brings no joy or satisfaction to Christian hearts but rather an extreme sense of heart-break.

Exclusivists resonate with Gary P. Stewart's words:

> It grieves me to think of the suffering that awaits those who reject or do not hear the Good News (see Luke 16:19-26). Among them are friends and members of my own family. I wish I could believe in their annihilation or conditional immortality or that God would save them in spite of themselves. But the Scriptures do not allow such a position. So I pray, trusting in the goodness and wisdom of god who knows the hearts of all men and women and whose discernment for outweighs my own. Who am I to question what He has set in place? I am the messenger, not the message or its drafter" (2000:379-80).

Our conviction of the biblical teachings of lostness and eternal separation from God should propel us to witness in the entire world. Christians cannot satisfied until the *ta ethne* (all peoples) of the world are in the Father's house.

Christians should approach adherents of other reli-

***gions and cults through respect, dialogue, love, and a
godly desire for them.*** This approach, while accepting and
loving, will be a winsome and courageous communication of
the Gospel of Jesus Christ as the one and only way for coming to God. Christians should seek points of contact with adherents of other religions and cults so as to communicate
more clearly the Gospel of Christ, which alone has the message of eternal life. Evangelical dialogue allows full access to
discussion on a meaningful basis without surrender of Christian truth.

Lesslie Newbigin asserts as to the purpose of dialogue
from the Christian viewpoint:

> The purpose of dialogue for the Christian is obedient
> witness to Jesus Christ, who is not the property of the
> church but the Lord of the church and of all people and
> who is glorified as the living Holy Spirit takes all that
> the Father has given to humankind - all people of eve-
> ry creed and culture - and declares it to the church as
> that which belongs to Christ as Lord. In this encounter
> the church is changed, the world is changed. and
> Christ is glorified (1995 Kindle Locations 2478-2481).

In seeking to respond to the commission (Matt 20:16-28),
Christians should avoid any statement of "triumphalism" that
dismisses any value or beauty in other religions. Christians
should recognize that some truth as well as falsehood exists
in the religions. The followers of these religions are created
in God's image and within his great desire for salvation.
Christians engage in witness to the followers of religions with
humility, sensitivity, gentleness, and respect (see Netland
2005: 16). Winfried Corduan concludes:

> The key to evangelism in a religiously plural world is to
> invite people to partake of the truth. It is not an exer-
> cise to entice people into an organization, the beliefs of
> which will then be gradually revealed to them. Nor is it
> a campaign to see who can promise the most on the
> marketplace of personal fulfillment. And it certainly is
> not a method of putting the Christian dish on the
> postmodern religious cafeteria display. Instead, it is
> the invitation to partake of God's one and only plan of
> salvation, and this must be clear (2002:237).

The gospel of Jesus Christ should be expressed in terms

most easily understood and accepted by the people addressed. The points of contact should be seriously searched and graciously used in all gospel proclamation. The end purpose of this dialogue with followers of religions must remain their conversion. *We seek contact so as to communicate the message of Jesus, the only Savior of humankind.*

Alan Tippett declares:

> The early church, at least in New Testament times, created no role of 'dialogist' so we cannot put this beside the preacher, apostle, evangelist, teacher and witness. However both the Lord and his followers did use the dialogical method in carrying out their functional roles. I see no reason why an evangelist, a teacher, or a witness should not use the dialogical approach in his evangelism, teaching or testifying, but the preacher and the apostle must reserve the right to make a monological proclamation as a word from the Lord. Our attitudes should always be humble and sympathetic, our forms should be a appropriate to the culture and generation to whom we speak in all things and we should remember we are there, not to establish ourselves, but to represent our Lord and to introduce men to Him. I agree with Beaver's personal opinion that dialogue is a form of witness consistent with the spirit of Christ and that is seems to meet the need of the times. Yet I believe the Christian participant in dialogue should direct his participation towards the evangelical goal, realizing of course that this requires the seal of the Holy Spirit (1969:48).

The only proper culmination of a biblically based theology of religions centers on loving, living, and evangelizing to the glory of God. We must share God's gospel with people and peoples everywhere. So far as we know from Scripture, Jesus Christ is the only chance they have. We long that they might know the peace that passes all understanding and that someday they will live with Jesus in Paradise. We also long that they have the wonderful experience of living and walking with Christ during their lifetimes.

Speaking strongly in the Exclusivist view, Sinclair B. Ferguson declares:

> But if this is our conviction [that no promise of salva-

tion outside of Christ is given in Scripture], it is empty and we ourselves rendered doubly inexcusable if we do not shift heaven and earth for the purpose of bringing the gospel to every creature in the missionary enterprise (2004:236).

Ott, Strauss, and Tennent sound this same conviction. They show that the usual way God saves people is through their hearing the gospel of Jesus Christ that someone shares with them. This fact, they continue, shouts the urgency of sharing the message. They then express the "true scandal of mission" saying:

> The true scandal of mission is not that evangelicals believe that Jesus is the only way of salvation but that many who claim to believe this are doing little or nothing to spread the gospel to lost people around the world. Paul's passion to preach the gospel controlled his life (Rom 9:1-4; 10:1; 13:18-21). If we have no reason to believe that any individual will spend eternity with God unless that person puts his or her faith in Christ, then mission becomes the most urgent task of the church and of every individual believer (Ott, Strauss, Tennent 2010:338).

An important aspect of the Christian witness and growth relates to the personal dimension as well as the informational. This fact indicates that the proper Christian response to the religions and those who follow them is personal living, corporate Christian service, and effective witnessing for Christ. John Newport declares that the greatest service we can render to the world lies in our being authentic followers of Jesus Christ, demonstrating his miraculous powers in our daily lives and services, and winsome testimony to his love and salvation (Newport 1989:413).

The entire concept of Christian living and witnessing and the close contact between the two is captured in the following words:

> The early Christians not only outthought, but also outlived and out died the pagans. If we are to authentically present the claims of the gospel to those of other religious beliefs, we must do the same. This means that our concern for justice and our faithfulness to God's commands must rival that of the committed Muslim.

> Our belief in agape love's superiority to Eastern com-
> passion must be demonstrated in unselfish service
> without racial discrimination. And our understand the
> respect for the Jewish tradition must show that we tru-
> ly appreciate our heritage. And then, we must honestly
> relate the experiences and relation that lie behind our
> actions (Newport 1989:412).

We remain convinced that Jesus is the only Savior, that the
Father desires the salvation of all persons, and that the Holy
Spirit is actively present in guiding and empowering all efforts to bring salvation to any who will repent. In keeping
with these convictions, we must be faithful, active, loving,
and dedicated persons who live their own faith and seek to
guide others to the blessed experience (see Newport 1978).

Conclusion

Every person concerned about and engaged in world evangelism should consider the imperative questions related to
Christianity and the non-Christian religions and cults. This
question, difficult as it may be, cannot be ignored. The only
biblical assurance we have is that faith in Christ, during
one's lifetime, will receive eternal life. Jesus Christ is, then,
the one and only Savior.

Only Jesus

CHAPTER 6

A CALL TO EVANGELICALS

The sobering statements in the forgoing pages set the stage for a desperate and imperative plea to Evangelical Christians. This call to Evangelicals constitutes the basic and underlying reason for this book. Understanding the various teachings concerning Christianity and the religions is important. *This book is, however, but another study if it does not significantly impact our actual personal and corporate efforts to guide men and women to personal faith in the Risen Lord.*

Evangelicals must remain true to the Word of God and refuse either to add t0 or to take out. God's teachings in the Bible provide the perfect guide for faith (what we believe) and practice (what we do). To fall into the abyss of any "wider-hope" theory or stumble in the "addition" falsity departs from the Master's commission. *In a day when the ideas of men are eroding the full teachings of the Maker of men and humans issue cries for tolerance in the most dogmatic of terms, Evangelicals must stand solidly and without flinching on the Word of God.*

If God's Word teaches that a wider-hope exists, we would welcome the teaching. If God's Word indicates that something in addition to and beyond simple faith in Christ is necessary for eternal life, we will embrace and abide by the teaching. The biblical truth is, however, that so far as we can ascertain from biblical teachings, God's Word supports only the conviction that S*alvation can be a reality only by a person's direct faith response, during his/her lifetime, to the message and person of the Historic, Risen Christ as presented in the Christian gospel.*

Since the forgoing statement expresses our fullest and most complete understanding of God's revelation, we must ask the basic and all-important question. What must Evangelical Christians do in light of the fact that the biblical teachings indicate that Jesus Christ is the only Savior and that apart from faith in him no person can reach the personal relationship with God that eventuates in eternal life? Answering this riveting question requires attention to the following guidelines:

- *Let us accept without flinching our best understanding of biblical truth.* We have accepted the interpretation that salvation is only in the one and only Savior Jesus Christ. We believe that the Bible is the Word of God, inerrant and infallible in all that it claims and teaches. It is, therefore imperative that we determine what it says, abide by what it enjoins, respond to it with joy, and share its message with people everywhere who perish without it. Without pride in our own faith, criticism of other religions, or condescension toward other faiths, we maintain our conviction in the truth of Christ as the one and only Savior for humankind.

- *Let us turn from the use of human logic or emotional expression of biblical teachings.* Many of the most damaging misunderstandings of Christian doctrine through history have resulted from the imposition of human logic on biblical truth. Other misinterpretations have sprung from the indiscriminate infusion of human emotions on divine decrees. While our logic and emotion may question biblical revelation, it behooves those who trust Scripture to remain with the divine revelation rather than the human adjustments.

  Grave dangers lurk in the possibilities of adding to or taking away from God's statement of reality. We call on Evangelicals, therefore, to remain staunch in the belief of and support for the truth of the Bible. We are convinced that this truth is captured in the position, *Only Jesus.*

- *Let us maintain our basic convictions of scriptural truth in the face of mounting criticism of authority and the growing relativity of our society.* Without pride or critical spirit, we must hold fast to our understanding of biblical truth. We hold these basic beliefs to be inviolate in relation to the teaching of Only Jesus

  ➢ That the inerrant Bible remains our guide and foundation. All other teachings must be judged in light of biblical truth

> That the Bible presents only the message that Jesus Christ is the one and only Savior for humankind

> That salvation in Christ comes through the experience of repentance and faith in the historical Christ entered into during a person's lifetime

> That God relates to humans on the basis of special revelation in which he shows himself to humans in grace

> That the Bible presents the experience of salvation as eternal, the future states of Heaven and Hell as everlasting, and gives believers complete assurance on all counts

Evangelicals would welcome a more open acceptance in the increasingly "tolerant" world of today. It becomes increasingly difficult to maintain the unpopular conviction of only one way of salvation. The firmness of belief in Christ as the only way confronts an increasingly rigid conviction of toleration. The people of our day do not openly accept the statement of Only Jesus. Evangelicals must seek God's approval; the acceptance of humans and the growing centrality of tolerance must remain of less importance.

- *Let us affirm the truth that the all-powerful God can execute other plans should that be in line with his nature and will.* We do not question the acts of God. If he offers salvation to others, we rejoice at the fact. The finite should not try to limit the infinite. The created should not dictate to the Creator. God can in ways we do not understand find ways to deal with those outside the voice of organized Christianity. *We must, however, remember that the Word of God makes no promise of any other way and we must live in the biblical light we have.*

- *Let us equally affirm that we must not rely on any hope for other ways of salvation.* Our commission remains to make disciples of all peoples. No human developed "wider-hope" possibility can relieve us of our responsibility to make his love known to all. The call for Christian missions sounds as loud and clear as in any period of history.

The pivotal convictions of "Only"Jesus" impel us to leave behind what Donald McGavran called "search theology" and embrace what he termed "harvest theology." We are not simply to overly invest ourselves with means to prepare the way to evangelism. We must never allow the proper ministries of healing, serving, and teaching to go undone. We are, however, called not just to provide the better ways of medicine, education, agriculture, cleaner water and air, and more justice social institutions. Our God-given opportunity is sharing the Good News with people everywhere and seeing them returning repentant and saved to the Father's home.

- *Let us faithfully remember that the beauty and glory of salvation relates to the best experience during lifetime as well as to the assurance of paradise in heaven.* The fact of endless separation from God in Hell is a strong motivation for evangelism. The truth of the glory of Heaven for eternity is likewise a major motive for guiding people to Christ.

We maintain our understanding that salvation has many dimensions and is not limited to the forgiveness of sins and escape from the horrors of Hell. The Bible shows that God's plan for humanity includes the social dimensions and the as the Church and the churches participate in God's Mission these followers of Christ must be aware of and active in meeting the full needs of humankind.

We must not neglect the teaching that salvation in Christ provides "everything we need for life and godliness through our knowledge of him who called us by his own glory and goodness" (2 Pet 1:3). The unsaved miss the glory of Heaven and suffer the terror of Hell. *They also, however, miss the experience of walking with Christ and knowing his love, care, provision, protection, and guidance in their daily experiences.* Piper eloquently expresses this truth saying: "What is at stake in denying the necessity to hear and believe the good news of Jesus is not only the escape from hell, but the enjoyment of all the benefits of knowing Christ. . . . there is no such thing as a "mere" escape from hell. Rescue from the worst and longest suffering can only be called "mere" by those who don't know what it is, or don't believe it's real. But implicit in the rescue from hell is the experience of praising God forever, and loving people forever, and enjoying creation forever, and creating beauty forever. All of this will be lost by everyone that the good news of Jesus does not reach. So what is at stake in diminishing the universal necessity of the gospel is the everlasting pleasures of people personally praising God, loving others, enjoying God's creation, and creating beauty. This is what people lose by not hearing and believing the gospel of Jesus" (2010: Kindle Edition 940).

- *Let us remain open to lovingly participate in dialogue with followers of other religions but at the same time maintain our understanding that conversion remains our objective.* We will not, in the effort to dialogue and establish more adequate relationship with others neither compromise our beliefs nor water down our commission.

We will maintain our stance of humility and sensitivity toward followers of other religions. We will willingly listen with a view to understanding and learning from followers of other religions. We will approach others with respect and acknowledge their personhood. Nothing of arrogant triumphalism will arise within our approaches. *We will, however, seek conversion from those to whom we take the saving message of Jesus Christ.*

These dialogues constitute more than searches for greater understanding of the others as important as that quest might be. Christians in dialogue remain committed to the truth of their faith and see in the dialogue opportunities to help others by sharing their faith in Jesus Christ. Leaving conversion out of the dialogue takes away the primary reason for the New Testament commission to "make disciples of all persons" (Matt 28:16-20).

Only Jesus

- *Let us allow our theological position to impel us to exert full efforts to share his love with all peoples.* We will live faithfully with our convictions and never compromise our beliefs that Jesus is the one and only Savior. The biblical teaching of Only Jesus remains a primary motivation for world evangelism and ministry (see Ellenberger 1991:226-27). Our only assurance is that those who trust Christ during their lifetimes will be saved.

Believers must, however, in order to be true to their beliefs, share the message of redemption with all. Little does it benefit humankind for God's followers to loudly profess their belief in the lost condition of unbelievers if these convicted Christians do nothing to spread the one message of salvation in Christ among the lost.

I am concerned about people named Rahner, Talbot, Pinnock, Sanders, Ferré, Hicks, Robertson, MacDonald, and Bell who hold to wider-hope theories. I am, however, far more deeply concerned about those of us who accept the biblical truth of *Only Jesus yet do so little about sharing this message with the lost. Is it not possible that our negligence in effective witness is the greatest liberalism of all?*

Acceptance of the truth, "Only Jesus" must drive us to the fields to serve with the Lord of the Harvest in the eternal reaping of the souls of those who respond to God's call and come to the experience of the Creator in salvation. The only proper response to these convictions is a vast sharing of this Good News with people everywhere. *The most alarming sin is not the liberal misinterpretation of biblical teaching but the Evangelical neglect of the responsibilities of effective and loving witness.*

Our theology is of little use if we do not engage in effective evangelism. *By effective evangelism I mean the service of leading men and women to become responsible, reproducing disciples of Jesus and incorporating them into responsible, reproducing congregations* (see Smith 1984:38-42; 2003:63-67). We should go far beyond these affirmations of correct biblical interpretation to the actual practice in evangelism. This study reaches its goal only as multiplying numbers of believers engage personally and congregationally in effective evangelism and church planting. Edmund Perry is obviously correct in saying that the major obstacle in the way of Christian missions to the other religions is not the other religions but the Christians themselves (1970:224).

My prayer is that we will remain firm in our acceptance of biblical truth without compromise or retreat. I am convinced, and I hope you too are convinced, of the truth of the statement:

> *Salvation can only be attained by a person's direct and conscious faith response, during his/her lifetime, to the message and person of the Historic, Risen Christ as presented in the Christian Gospel.*

The question is now, what we going to do about this truth? **Our only proper response to the truth of "Only Jesus" is the proclamation, without hesitation or neglect, with love and compassion, the Word of God to every person around the world.**

Only Jesus

Sources

Adams, M. M. 1975. "Hell and the Justice of God." *Religious Studies 11 (1975): 433-47.*

_____. 1993. "The Problem of Hell: A Problem of Evil for Christians." In *A Reasoned Faith,* ed. E. Stump. Ithaca, NY: Cornell University Press.

_____. 1999. *Horrendous Evils and the Goodness of God.* Ithaca, NY: Cornell University Press.

Allen, Ken. Nd, "Basic Doctrines of Universalism" http://www.auburn.edu/~allenkc/cudoctrine.html.

Aldwinckle, Russell F. 1982. *Jesus—A Savior The Savior.* Macon Ga.: Mercer University Press.

Anderson, Gerald. 1993. In *The Good News of the Kingdom: Mission Theology for the Third Millennium.* Charles Van Engen, Dean Gilliland, and Paul Pierson eds. Maryknoll, NY: Orbis.

Anderson, G. H. and T. F. Stransky, eds. 1994. *Faith Meets Faith,* Mission Trends No. 5. Grand Rapids: Eerdmans.

Anderson , J. N. D. 1970. *Christianity and Comparative Religion.* Downers Grove, IL: InterVarsity Press.

Anderson, Sir Norman. 1971. *Christianity and Comparative Religion.* Downers Grove, IL: InterVarsity Press.

_____. 1984. *Chrisitianity and World Religions.* Downers Grove, IL: InterVarsity Press.

Arnold, Clinton E. 1996. *The Colossian Syncretism: The interface between Christianity and folk belief at Colosse.* Grand Rapids: Baker Acadamic Books.

_____. 1997. *3 Crucial Questions about Spiritual Warfare.* Grand Rapids: Baker Academic Books.

Augustine, Saint. 1972. *Concerning the City of God Against the Pagans,* Translated Henry Bettenson. London: Penguin.

Baker, David W., ed. 2004. *Biblical Faith and Other Religions: An Evangelical Assessment.* Grand Rapids: Kregel Publications.

Ballou, Hosea. 1986. *Treatise on Atonement.* Skinner House.

Bauckham, Richard J. 1979, "Universalism—A historical survey," *Themelios* 4, 2 (January 1979): 48-53.

Only Jesus

Barnett, Mike and Pocock, Michael eds. 2005. *The Centrality of Christ in Contemporary Missions.* EMS Series no. 12. Pasadena, CA: William Carey Library.

Barth, Karl. 1936-1962. *Church Dogmatics* Ed. Groffrey W. Bromley and Thomas F. Torrance. Edinburgh: T. and T. Clark.

_____. 1960. *The Humanity of God.* Atlanta: John Knox Press.

Beale, Gregory K. 2004. "The Revelation on Hell," in *Hell Under Fire: Modern Scholarship Reinvents Eternal Punishment.* Grand Rapids: Zondervan.

Bell, Rob. 2011. *Love Wins: A Book About Heaven, Hell, and the Fate of Every Person who Ever Lived.* New York: HarperCollins.

Beougher, Timothy K. 1998. "Are All Doomed to Be Saved? The Rise of Modern Universalism." *The Southern Baptist Journal of Theology* 2, 2 (Summer 1998): 6-25.

Beyerhouse, Peter. 1971. "Indigenous Churches," in *Concise Dictionary of the Christian World Mission*, ed. Stephen Neill, Gerald H. Anderson, and John Goodwin. Nashville, TN: Abingdon Press.

_____. 1972. *Shaken Foundations.* Grand Rapids: Zondervan Press.

_____. 1975. "Possession and Syncretismin Biblical Perspective," in *Christopaganism or Indigenous Christianity?*, ed. Tetsunao Yammori and Charles R. Tabor. Pasadena, CA: William Carey Library.

Bishops of the Netherlands, 1967. *A New Catechism: Catholic Faith for Adults.* Herder and Herder.

Block, Daniel I. 2004. "The Old Testament on Hell," in *Hell Under Fire: Modern Scholarship Reinvents Eternal Punishment.* Grand Rapids: Zondervan.

Blum, Edwin A. 1979. "Shall you not surely die" *Themelios* 4, 2 (January 1979): 58-61.

Boutin, Maurice. 1983. "Anonymous Christianity: A Paradigm for Interreligious Encounter" *Journal of Ecumenical Studies* (Fall 1983): 6-9.

Boettner, Loraine. 1954. *The Reformed Doctrine of Pre-Destination.* Grand Rapids: Eerdmans.

Bosch, David J. 1991. *Transforming Mission: Paradign Shifts in Theology of Mission.* American Society of Missiology Series No. 16. Maryknoll, NY: Orbis Books.

Braaten, Carl R. 1980. "Who Do We Say That He Is? On the Uniqueness and Universality of Jesus Christ," *Occasional Bulletin of Missionary Research* (January 1980): 5-7.

Sources

_____. 1994. "The Uniqueness and Universality of Jesus Christ," in *Faith Meets Faith,* Mission Trends, No. 5, ed. G. H. Anderson and T. F. Stransky. Grand Rapids: Eerdmans.

Burk, Denny. March 14, 2011. "Revising Hell Into the Heterodox Mainstream?" http://dennyburk.com/revising-hell-into-the-heterodox-mainstream.

Carson, D. A. 1996. *The Gagging of God: Christianity Confronts Pluralism.* Grand Rapids: Zondervan.

_____. 2000. *The Difficult Doctrine of the Love of God.* Wheaton, IL: Crossway.

Cate, Patrick. 2005. "The Uniqueness of Christ and Missions," in In *The Centrality of Christ in Contemporary Missions,* ed Mike Barnett and Michael Pocock, EMS Series no. 12. William Carey Library.

Chancellor, James D. 1994. "Christ and Religious Pluralism," *Review and Expositor* 91 (1994): 535-47.

Clark, David K. 1991. "Is Special Revelation Necessary for Salvation," in *Through No Fault of Their Own*, ed. William V. Crockett and James G. Sigountos. Grand Rapids: Baker Book House.

Clooney, Francis. 1989. "Christianity and World Religions: Religion, Reason, and Pluralism," *Religious Studies Review* 15 (July 1989):200.

Cobb, John Jr. 2002. *Christian Faith and Religious Diversity: Mobilization for the Human Family.* Minneapolis: Fortress Press.

Conn, Harvey. 1991."Do Other Religions Save?" in *Through No Fault of Their Own*, ed. William V. Crockett and James G. Sigountos. Grand Rapids: Baker Book House.

Corduan, Winfried. 1998a. "Budda, Shiva, and Mohammad: Theistic Faith in Other Religions?" *The Southern Baptist Journal of Theology* 2, 2 (Summer 1998): 40-49.

_____. 1998b. *Neighboring Faith.* Downers Grave, IL: InterVarsity Press.

_____. 2000. "Buddha, Shiva, and Muhammad," in *Who Will Be Saved? Defending the Biblical Understanding of God, Salvation, & Evangleism,* ed. By Paul R. House & Gregory A. Thornbury. Wheaton, IL: Crossway Books.

_____. 2002. *A Tapestry of Faiths: The Common Threads Between Christianity & World Religions.* Downers Grove, IL: InterVarsity Press.

Copeland, E. Luther. 1999. *A New Meeting of the Religions.* Baylor University Press.

Cox, Samuel. 1899. *Salvater Mundi or Is Christ the Savior of All Men.* London: Kegan

Only Jesus

Craig, W. L. 1987. *The Only Wise God: The Compatibility of Divine Fore-knowledge and Human Freedom*. Grand Rapids: Baker Book House.

_____. 1988. "Politically Incorrect Salvation" in *Christian Apologetics in the Postmodern World*, ed. Timothy R. Phillips and Dennis Okholm. Downers Grove, IL: InterVarsity Press.

_____. 1989. "No Other Name': A Middle Knowledge Perspective on the Exclusivity of Salvation through Christ." *Faith and Philosophy* 6 (1989):172-88.

_____. 1995. "Middle Knowledge and Christian Exclusivism." *Sophia* 34 (1995):120-39.

Crisp, Oliver. 2003a. "Divine Retribution: A Defense." *Sophia* 42(2003): 36-53.

_____. 2003b "Augustinean Universalism." *International Journal for Philosophy of Religion* 53 (2003): 127-45.

_____. 2003c. "On Barth's Denial of Universalism." *Themelios* 29 (2003): 18-29.

_____. 2011. "I Do Teach It, but I Also Do Not Teach It: The Universalism of Karl Barth (1886–1968)" in *All shall be well: Explanations in Universalism and Christian Theology, from Origen to Molmann*. Ed. Gregory MacDonald. Eugene, OR: Wipf and Stock Publishers.

Crockett, William V. and Sigountos, James G. eds. 1991. *Through No Fault of Their Own*. Grand Rapids: Baker Book House.

Demarest, Bruce. 1982. *General Revelation*. Grand Rapids: Zondervan, 1982.

DeRose, Keith. 1999. "Universalism and the Bible," http://pantheon.yale.edu/%7Ekd47/univ.htm.

Driver, Tom F. 1988. "The Case for Pluralism," in *The Myth of Christian Uniqueness: Toward a Pluralistic Theology of Religions*. ed. John Hick and Paul F. Knitter. Maryknoll, New York: Orbis Books.

D'Costa, Gavin . 1986. "The Pluralist Paradigm in Christian Theology of Religions," *The Scottish Journal of Theology* 39 (1986): 81.

Dupis, Jacques. 1997. *Toward A Christian Theology of Religious Pluralism*. (Maryknoll, NY: Orbis Books.

Eddy, Paul. 1993. "John Hick's Theological Pilgrimage," in Proceedings of the Wheaton College Theology Conference, Vol. 1 *The Challenge of Religious Pluralism: An Evangelical Analysis and Response*.

Edwards, David and Stott, John. 1988, *Evangelical Essentials: A Liberal-Evangelical Dialogue*. Downers Grove: InterVarsity Press.

Sources

Edwards. Jonathan. 2001. "The Justice of God in the Damnation of Sinners," in Sermons and Discourses 1734-1738, vol. 19, *The Works of Jonathan Edwards*. New Haven: Yale University Press.

Ellenberger, John D. 1991."Is Hell a Proper Motivation for Missions?" In *Through No Fault of Their Own,* ed. Crockett and Sigountos. Grand Rapids: Baker Book House.

Ellul, Jacques. 1981. *Perspective on Our Age: Jacques Ellul Speaks on His Life and Work.* Toronto: Canadian Broadcasting Corporation.

Erickson, Millard. 1975. "Hope for those who haven't heard? Yes, but . . . "*Evangelical Missions Quarterly* 11, 2 (April 1975): 122-128.

_____. 1991. "The State of the Question," in *Through No Fault of Their Own*, ed. William V. Crockett and James G. Sigountos. Grand Rapids: Baker Book House.

_____. 1993. *The Evangelical Heart and Mind.* Grand Rapids: Baker Books

_____. 1994. *Where Is Theology Going? Issues and Perspectives in the Future of_Theology.* Grand Rapids: Baker Book House.

_____. 1996. *How Shall They Be Saved?* Grand Rapids: Baker Book House.

_____. 1998. "The State of the Unevangelized and Its Missionary Implications," in *Missiology: An Introduction to the Foundations, History, and Strategies of World Missions*, ed. Mark Terry, Ebbie Smith, Justice Anderson. Broadman & Holman.

Executive Committee, SBC. 1993. *Annual of the Southern Baptist Convention.* Nashville: Executive Committee, SBC.

Fackre, Gabriel. 1995. "Divine Providence," in *What About Those Who Have Never Heard*? ed. John Sanders. Downers Grove: InterVarsity Press.

Ferré, Nels F. S. 1947. *Evil and the Christian Faith*. New York: Harper & Brothers.

_____. 1951. *The Christian Understanding of God.* New York: Harper & Brothers

_____. 1963. "Universalism: Pro and Con," Christianity Today 7 (March 1, 1963).

Frame, John M. 2001. *No Other God: A Response to Open Theism.* Philipsburg, NJ: Presbyterian and Reformed Book Company.

Fudge, Edward W. 1982 rev. 1994. *The Fire that Consumes: the Biblical Case for Conditional immortality,* ed. Peter Cousins, rev. ed. Paternoster.

Only Jesus

Fudge, Edward and Peterson, Robert A. 2000. *Two Views of Hell: A Biblical & Theological Dialogue.* Downers Grove, IL: InterVarsity Press.

Garrett, James Leo. 2000. *Systematic Theology: Biblical, Historical, and Evangelical* 2d ed. 2 vols. (North Richland Hills, TX: BIBAL Press.

Geivett, R. Douglas and Phillips, W. Gary. 1995. "A Particularist View: An Evidentialist Approach" in *More Than One Way?* Ed. Okholm, Dennis L. &. Phillips, Timothy R. Zondervan (This book published in 1996 as *Four View on Salvation in a Pluralistic World*).

Geivett, R. Douglas and Pinnock, Clark. 1998. "'Misgivings' and 'Openness': A Dialogue on Inclusiviism Between R. Douglas Geivett and Clark Pinnock" *The Southern Baptist Journal of Theology* 2, 2 (Summer 1998): 26-39.

George, Timothy. 2000. *Amazing Grace: God's Initiative—Our Response.* Nashville.TN: LifeWay Press.

Gilkey, Langdon. 1987. "Plurality and Its Theological Implications," in *The Myth of Christian Uniqueness: Toward a Pluralistic Theology of Religions,* ed John Hick and Paul F. Knitter. Maryknoll, NY: Orbis Books.

Graham, Billy. 1993. "Of Angels, Devils, and Messages from God." *Time* (November 15, 1993); 74.

Griggs, Tom. "'Jesus Is Victor': Passing the Impasse of Barth on Universalism." *Scottish Journal of Theology* 62 (2007) 196–212.

Griffiths, Paul J. ed. 1990. *Christianity Through Non-Christian Eyes* (Fatih Meets Faith Series). Maryknoll: NY: Orbis books.

Grounds, Vernon C. 1981. "The Final State of the Wicked, *"Journal of the Evangelical Theological Society* (September 1981): 215.

Gulley, Philip and Mulholland, James. 2003. *If Grace Is True: Why God will Save Every Person.* New York: HarperCollins Publishers.

MacDonald, Gregory (2011-01-01). "All Shall Be Well": Explorations in Universal Salvation and Christian Theology, from Origen to Moltmann (p. 400). Cascade Books, an imprint of Wipf and Stock Publishers. Kindle Edition.

Hackett, Stuart C. 1984. *The Reconstruction of the Chrristian Revelation Claim.* Grand Rapids: Baker Books, Academic.

Hanson, J [John] W [Wesley] 1899. *Universalism the Prevailing Doctrine of the Christian Church during its First Five Hundred Years.* Boston and Chicago: Universalists Publishing House.

Hall, Lindsey. 2011. "Hell and the God of Love Universalism in the Philosophy of John Hick (1922–)" in *"All Shall Be Well": Explorations in Universal Salvation and Christian Theology, from Origen to Molt-*

mann. Cascade Books, an imprint of Wipf and Stock Publishers. Kindle Edition.

Hardon, John A. 1981, *The Catholic Catechism: A Contemporary Catechism of the Teachings of the Catholic Church.* Doubleday.

Henry, Carl F. H. 1949. *Giving A Reason for Our Hope.* Boston: W. A. Wilde.

_____. 1983. *God, Revelation and Authority,* 6 vols. Vol. VI. Waco, TX: Word.

_____. 1991. "Is It Fair," in *Through No Fault of Their Own: The Fate of Those Who Have Never Heard,* ed. W. Crockett and J. Sigountos

_____. 2000. "The Living God of the Bible" in *Who Will Be Saved?* Ed. Paul R. House & Gregory A. Thornbury. Wheaton, IL: Crossway Books.

Heim, S. Mark. 1995. *Salvations: Truth and Difference in Religion.* Maryknoll, New York: Orbis Books.

Hesselgrave, J. and Rommen, Edward. 1989. *Contextualization: Meanings, Methods, and Models.* Grand Rapids: Baker Book House.

Hick, John. 1968. *Christianity at the Centre.* London: Macmillan.

_____. 1973. "Jesus and the World Religions," in *God and the Universe of Faith.* London: Collins.

_____. 1977. "Jesus and the World Religions," in *The Myth of God Incarnate,* ed. John Hick (London: SCM).

_____. 1980a. *God Has Many Names.* Philadelphia: Westminster Press.

_____. 1980b. "Whatever Path Men Choose Is Mine," in *Christianity and Other Religions*, ed John Hick and Brian Hebblethwaithe. Philadelphia: Judson Press.

_____. 1980c. "Jesus and the World Religions," in *Christianity and Other Religions*, ed John Hick and Brian Hebblethwaithe. Philadelphia: Judson Press.

_____. 1982. "Is There Only One Way to God," *Theology.* Jan 1982: 124.

_____. 1985. *Problems of Religious Pluralism*. New York: St. Martin's Press

_____. 1987. "The Non-Absoluteness of Christianity," in *The Myth of Christian Uniqueness: Toward a Pluralistic Theology of Religions,* ed John Hick and Paul F. Knitter. Maryknoll, NY: Orbis Books.

_____. 1989. *An Interpretation of Religion.* New Haven: Yale University Press.

Only Jesus

_____. 1993. *Disputed Questions in Theology and the Philosophy of Religion* (New Haven, Conn: Yale University Press.

_____. 1995. *The Rainbow of Faiths.* London: SCM.

_____. 1999. *The Fifth Dimension.* Oxford: Oneworld.

Hick, John and Hebblethwaithe. Brian. 1980. *Christianity and Other Religions*, ed John Hick and Brian Hebblethwaithe. Philadelphia: Judson Press.

Hick, John and Knitter, Paul F. 1987. *The Myth of Christian Uni*queness, ed. John Hick and Paul F. Knitter (Maryknoll, New York: Orbis Books.

Hodge, Charles 1940, *Systematic Theology*, 3 vols. Grand Rapids: Eerdmans.

Hocking, William Ernest. 1932. *Re-Thinking Mission: a Laymen's Inquiry After One Hundred Years.* New York: Harper.

Hogue, James V. and Smith, Ebbie C. 1989. *Christianity Faces a Pluralistic World.* Ft. Worth, Tx: Christian Literary Publications.

House, Paul R. 1998. "Editoral: Biblical Theology and the Inclusivist Challenge." *The Southern Baptist Journal of Theology* 2,2 (Summer 1998): 2-5.

House, Paul R. and Thornbury, Gregory A. 2000. *Who Will Be Saved? Defending the Biblical Understanding of Tod, Salvation, & Evangelism.* Wheaton, IL: Crossway Books.

Jüngel, Eberhard. *Karl Barth: A Theological Legacy.* Translated by Garrett E. Paul. Philadelphia: Westminster, 1986.

Kane, Herbert J. 1982. *Understanding Christian Missions*, 2d ed. Grand Rapids, Baker. (first published 1974).

Kärkkäinen, Veli-Matti. 2003. *An Introduction to the Theology of Religions: Biblical, Historical, and Contemporary Perspectives.* InterVarsity Press.

_____. 2004. *Trinity and Religious Pluralism: The Doctrine of the Trinity in Christian Theology of Religions.* Ashgate Publishing Company.

Klostermaier, Klaus. 1967. "Dialogue—The Words of God," in *Inter-Religious Dialogue,* ed. Herbert Jai Singh. Bangalore: the Christian Institute for the Study of Religion and Society.

_____. 1971. "Hindu-Christian Dialogue" in *Dialogue Between Men of Living Faiths,* ed. Stanley J. Samartha. Geneva: World Council of Churches.

Knitter, Paul K. 1985. *No Other Name?* Maryknoll, NY: Orbis Books.

Sources

_____. 1987. "Toward A Liberation Theology on Religions in in *The Myth of Christian Uni*queness, ed. John Hick and Paul F. Knitter. Maryknoll, New York: Orbis Books.

_____. 2005 *Introducing Theologies of Religion.* Maryknoll , New York: Orbis Books.

_____. 2009. *Without Buddha I Could Not Be A Christian.* Oxford: One-World.

Kniter, Paul. Ed. 2005. *The Myth of Religious Superiority: A Multifaith Exploration.* Maryknoll, NY: Orbis Books.

Kraemer, Hendrick. 1938. *The Christian Message in a Non-Christian World.* Grand Rapids: Kregel Publishing Co.

_____ . 1956. *Religion and the Christian Faith*. Philadelphia: Westminster Press.

_____. 1962. *Why Christianity of All Religions?,* Philadelphia: Westminster Press.

Küng, Hans. 1966. *Freedom Today.* New York: Sheed & Ward.

Lewis, James R. and Travis, William G. 1991. *Religious Traditions of the World.* Grand Rapids: Zondervan.

Lindsell, Harold. 1949. *A Christian Philosophy of Mission.* Wheaton: Van Kampen Press,

_____. 1965. "Universalism Today: Part Two," *Bibliotheca Sacra* 122 (January-March 1965).

Little, Christopher. 2000. *The Revelation of God among the Unevangelized.* Pasadena, CA: William Carey Library.

_____. 2002. "Toward Solving the Problem of the Unevangelized," *Africa Journal of Evangelical Theology* 2002 21 (1): 45-62

Ludlow, Morwenna. *Universal Salvation: Eschatology in the Thought of Gregory of Nyssa and Karl Rahner.* Oxford University

Luther, Martin. 1998. *Galatians* in *The Crossway Classic Commentaries,* ed. Alister McGrath and J. I. Packer. Wheaton, IL: Crossway Books

Lutzer, Erwin W. 2000. "The Uniqueness of Christianity over Other Religions," in *The Fundamentals for the Twenty-First Century,* ed. Mal Couch. Grand Rapids: Kregel.

Marshall, I. H. 2000. "Does the New Testament Teach Universal Salvation?" In *Called to One Hope: Perspectives on the Life to Come.* Ed. J. Colwell. Carlisle: Paternoster.

Only Jesus

_____. 2003. "The New Testament Does *Not* Teach Universal Salvation." In *Universal Salvation? The Current Debate.* Ed. R. A. Parry and C. H. Partridge. Carlisle: Paternoster (Eerdmans).

MacDonald, Gregory. 2006, 2008. *The Evangelical Universalist.* Eugene, Oregan, London: Wipf & Stock, Society for Promoting Christian Knowledge.

_____. Ed. 2011. *All shall be well*: *Explanations in Universalism and Christian Theology, from Origen to Molmann.* Eugene, OR: Wipf and Stock Publishers

McGrath, Alister E. 1995. "A Particularist View: A Post-Enlightenment Approach," in *More Than One Way?* Ed. Okholm, Dennis L. &. Phillips, Timothy R. Zondervan (This book published in 1996 as *Four View on Salvation in a Pluralistic World.*

McQuilkin, Robertson. 1994. *The Great Omission.* Grand Rapids: Baker Book House.

Moo, Douglas J. 1991. "Romans 2: Saved Apart from the Gospel?" in *Through No Fault of Their Own*, ed. William V. Crockett and James G. Sigountos. Grand Rapids: Baker Book House.

_____. 2004. "Paul on Hell," in *Hell Under Fire,* eds. Christopher W. Morgan and Robert A. Peterson. Zondervan.

Moody, Dale. 1981. *The Word of Truth.* Grand Rapids: Eerdmans.

Morgan, Christopher W. and Peterson, Robert A. eds. 2004a. *Hell Under Fire.* Grand Rapids: Zondervan.

Morgan, Christopher W. and Peterson, Robert A. eds. 2004b. *Is Hell for Real or Does Everyone Go to Heaven?.* Grand Rapids: Zondervan.

_____. 2008. *Faith Comes by Hearing: A Response to Inclusivism.* Downers Grove, IL; IVP Academic.

Morgan, Christopher W. 2008. "Inclusivism and Exclusivism" in *Faith Comes by Hearing: A Response to Inclusivism.* Eds. Morgan, Christopher W. and Peterson, Robert A.

Murray, George W. 2005. "Is Jesus Christ Really the Only Way? In *The Centrality of Christ in Contemporary Missions,* ed Mike Barnett and Michael Pocock, EMS Series no. 12. William Carey Library.

Nash, Ronald H. 1994. *Is Jesus the Only Savior?* Grand Rapids: Zondervan.

_____. 1995a. "Restrictivism," in *What About Those Who Have Never Heard*? ed. John Sanders. Downer Grove: InterVarsity Press.

_____. 1995b. "Response to Fackre," in *What About Those Who Have Never Heard*? ed. John Sanders. Downer Grove: InterVarsity Press.

Neill, Stephen C. 1961. *Christian Faith and the Other Faiths. Oxford.*

Sources

Netland, Harold A. 1987. "Exclusivism, Tolerance, and Truth," *Missiology* (April 1987): 77-78.

_____. 1991. *Dissonant Voices: Religious Pluralism and the Question of Truth.* Vancouver, BC: Regent College Publishing.

_____. 1995. "Introduction," in *Christianity and the Religions: A Biblical Theology of World Religions,* eds. Edward Rommen and Harold Netland, Evangelical Missiological Society Series No. 2. William Carey Library.

_____. 1995. "Application: Mission in a Pluralistic World," in *Christianity and the Religions: A Biblical Theology of World Religions,* eds. Edward Rommen and Harold Netland, Evangelical Missiological Society Series No. 2. William Carey Library.

_____. 2001. *Encountering Religious Pluralism: the Challenge to Christian Truth and Mission.* Downers Grove, IL: InterVarsity.

_____. 2005 "Mission and Jesus in a Global World: Mission as Retrieval" in *the Centrality of Christ in Contemporary Missions*, eds. Barnett and Pocock, Evangelical Missiological Society Series no. 12.

_____. 2010. "Religious Pluralisjm and the Question of Truth," in *Biblical Faith and Other Religions: An Evangelical Assessment,* ed. David W. Baker.

Newbigin, Lesslie. 1995 *The Open Secret:* (Kindle Edition).

Newport, John P. 1978. *Christ and the New Consciousness.* Nashville: Broadman Press.

_____. 1989. *Life's Ultimate Issues.* Dallas, TX: Word.

Nicole, Roger. 1979. "One Door and Only One," *Wherever* 4 (1979): 3.

Nicholls, Bruce J. 1979. "The Exclusiveness and Inclusiveness of the Gospel," *Themelios* 4, 2 (January 1979):62-68.

_____. 1994. "Introduction, in *The Unique Christ in Our Pluralist World.* Ed Bruce J. Nicholls. Grand Rapids, MI: Baker Books.

Nicholls, Bruce J. ed. 1994. *The Unique Christ in Our Pluralist World.* Grand Rapids, MI: Baker Books.

Nigel M. de S Cameron, Ed. 1992. *Universalism and the Doctrine of Hell: Papers Presented at the Fourth Edinburgh Conference on Christian Dogmatics.* Grand Rapids: Baker.

Noll, Mark A. and Wells, David F. 1988. *Christian Faith and Practice in the Modern World: Theology from an Evangelical Point of View.* Grand Rapids: Eerdmans.

Only Jesus

Olson, C. Gordon. 1998. *What in the World Is God Doing?* Cedar Knowlls, NJ: Global Gospel Publishers.

Okholm, Dennis L. &. Phillips, Timothy R. eds. 1995. *More Than One Way?* Grand Rapids: Zondervan (this book republished in 1996 as *Four Views on Salvation in a Pluralistic World*)

Onica, Paul. 2001. "Milestones: A Survey of Baptismal Regeneration," *Affirmation & Critique.* April 2001:51-57.

Origen. 1965. *Contra Celsum,* trans. Henry Chadwick. Cambridge: Cambridge University Press.

Orr, James. 1987, *The Christian View of God and the World.* New York: Charles Scribner's Sons.

Ott, Craig, Strauss, Stephen J. with Tennent Timothy C. *Encountering Theology of Mission: Biblical Foundations, Historical Developments, and Contemporary Issues.* Grand Rapids: Baker Academic, 2010.

Pachuau, Lalsangkima. 2000. "Missiology in a Pluralistic World: the Place of Mission Study in Theological Education," *The International Review of Mission* 89/No. 355 (October 2000): 539-555.

Packer, J. I. 1965. "All Men Won't Be Saved, "*Eternity* 16 (November 1965).

_____. 1967. "Universalism and Evangelism," in *One Race, One Gospel, One Task: Vol 2* ed. Carl F. H. Henry and W. Stanley Mooneyham. Minneapolis: World Wide Publications.

_____. 1986. "Good Pagans" and God's Kingdom, "*Christianity Today* 30, 1 January 17, 1986

_____. 1998. *Celebrating the Saving Work of God.* Carlisle: Paternoster.

_____. 2004a. "Universalism: Will Everyone Ultimately Be Saved?" in *Hell Under Fire*, ed. Morgan and Peterson. Grand Rapids: Zondervan.

_____. 2004b "Does Everyone Go to Heaven? In *Is Hell for Real or Does Everyone Go to Heaven?,* ed. Christiopher W. Morgan and Robert A. Peterson.

Panikkar, Raimundo. 1981. *The Unknown Christ of Hinduism.* London: Darton, Longman and Todd.

_____. 1987, "The Jordan, the Tiber, and the Ganges," in *The Myth of Christian Uniqueness,* ed. John Hick and Paul F. Knitter. Maryknoll, New York: Orbis Books.

Parry, Robin A. and. Partridge, Christopher H. 2003. "Introduction," *Universal Salvation: The Current Debate,* ed. Robin A. Parry and Christopher H. Partridge (Grand Rapids: Eerdmans).

Patrides, C. A. 1967. "The Salvation of Satan," *Journal of the History of Ideas.* 28 (October-December).

Sources

Perry, Edward. 1970. *The Gospel in Dispute: The kCC of Christian Faith to Other Missionary Religions.* New York: Doubleday and Company.

Peterson, Robert A. 1995. *Hell on Trial: the Case for Eternal Punishment.* Philipsburg, NJ: Presbyterian and Reformed Book Company.

_____. 2008. "Inclusivism versus Exclusivism on Key Biblical Texts," in " in *Faith Comes by Hearing: A Response to Inclusivism.* Ed Morgan, Christopher W. and Peterson, Robert A.

Phillips, Timothy. 1991. "Hell: A Christological Reflection," in *Through No Fault of Their Own?.* Ed. Crockett, William V. and Sigountos, James G. Baker Books.

Phillips, W. Gary. 1992. "Evangelicals and Pluralism: Current Options," in *Proceedings of the Wheaton Theological Conference.*

_____. 1994. "Evangelical Pluralism: A Singular Problem," *Bibliothneca Sacra* 151 (April-June).

Pierson, Arthur T. 1886. *The Crisis Missions.* New York: Robert Carter.

Pierson, Steven J. 2000. "Dialogue." In *Evangelical Dictionary or World Missions*, ed. A. Scott Moreau. Grand Rapids: Baker Books.

Piper, John. 1983. "How Does a Sovereign God Love?" *Reformed Journal* 33 (April 1983).

_____. 2002. *Counted Righteous in Christ.* Wheaton, IL: Crossway Books.

_____. 2010. *Jesus: The Only Way to God--Must You Hear the Gospel to be Saved?* (Kindle Location 80). Baker Books. Kindle Edition.

Pinnock, Clark. 1987. "Fire, Then Nothing," *Christianity Today* 31 (March 20, 1987): 40-41.

_____. 1988. "The Finality of Jesus Christ in a World of Religions," in *Christian Faith and Practice in the Modern World: Theology from an Evangelical Point of View*, ed. Mark A. Noll and David F. Wells. Grand Rapids: Eerdmans.

_____. 1990a. "The Destruction of the Finally Impenitent," *Chriswell Theological Review* 4 (1900); 246-47.

_____. 1990b. "Toward an Evangelical Theology of Religions," Journal of the "Evangelical Theological Society (JETS) 33.3 (June 1990), 359-368.

_____. 1991. "Acts 4:12—No Other Name Under Heaven," in *Through No Fault of Their Own*, ed. William V. Crockett and James G. Sigountos. Grand Rapids: Baker Book House.

_____. 1992. *A Wideness in God's Mercy: The Finality of Jesus Christ in a World of Religions.* Grand Rapids: Zondervan.

Only Jesus

_____. 1995 "An Inclusivist View," in in *More Than One Way?* Ed. Okholm, Dennis L. &. Phillips, Timothy R. Zondervan (This book published in 1996 as *Four View on Salvation in a Pluralistic World*)

Pinnock, Clark H. and Brow, Robert C. 1994. *Unbounded Love.* Downers Grove: InterVarsity Press.

Pinnock, Clark, Rice, Richard, Sanders, John, Hasker, William, and Basinger, David. 1994. *The Openness of God.* Downers Grove: InterVarsity Press.

Plantinga, Richard J. 2010. "God So Loved the World: Theological Reflections on Religious Plurality in the History of Christianity," In *Biblical Faith and Other Religions: An Evangelical Assessment*, ed. David W. Baker

Platt, Albert T. 2000. "In A Pagan World: The Mandate for Evangelism and Missions," in *The Fundamentals for the Twenty-First Century,* ed. Mal Couch. Grand Rapids: Kregel.

Punt, Neal. 1980. *Unconditional Good News: Toward an Understanding of Biblical Universalism.* Eerdmans Publishing Company.

Pusey, E. B. 1888. *What is of Faith as to Everlasting Punishment?* London: Walter Smith and Innes.

Race, Alan. 1982. *Christians and Religious Pluralism.* Orbis Books.

Ramm, Bernard. 1964, "Will All Men Be Finally Saved?" *Eternity* 15, 8 (August 1964): 22-23.

Rahner, Karl. 1979. "The One Christ and the Universality of Salvation," in *Theological Investigations,* Vol. 16, trans. David Morland. London: Darton, Longman, and Todd.

_____. 1980. "Christianity and the Non-Christian Religions," *in Christianity and the Other Religions: Selected Readings*, ed. John Hick and Brian Hebblethwaite. Philadelphia: Fortress Press.

Robinson, J.A.T. 1949. "Universalism—Is it Heretical?' *Scottish Journal of Theology* 2:2 (June 1940):139-155.

_____. 1950. *In the End God: A Study of the Christian Doctrine of the Last Thiings (London: James Clarke).*

Rommen, Edward and Netland, Harold, eds. 1995. *Christianity and the Religions: A Biblical Theology of World Religions.* No 2 Evangelical Missiological Society Series. William Carey Library.

Reitan, E. 2001. "Universalism and Autonomy: Towards a Comparative Defense of Universalism" *Faith and Philosophy* 18 (2001):222-40.

Sources

_____. 2003. "Human Freedom and the Impossibility of Eternal Damnation." In *Universal Salvation? The Current Debate,* ed. R. A. Parry ad C. H. Partridge. Carlisle: Paternoster (Grand Rapids: Eerdmans).

Ruokanen, Mikka 1992. *The Catholic Doctrine of Non-Christian Religions According to the Second Vatican Council.* (Leiden: E. J. Brill.

Runzo, Joseph 1988. "God, Commitment, and Other Faiths: Pluralism vs. Relativism," *Faith and Philosophy* 5 (1988): 351.

Samartha, Stanley J. 1987. "The Cross and the Rainbow: Christ in a Multireligious Culture" in *The Myth of Christian Uniqueness,* ed. John Hick and Paul F, Knitter. Maryknoll, NY: Orbis Books.

_____, 1988. "   " *The International Review of Missions.* (July 1988): 315.

Sanders, John. 1988. "Is Belief in Christ Necessary for Salvation?" *Evangelical Mission Quarterly* (1988): 259.

_____. 1988. "The Finality of Jesus Christ in a World of Religions," in *Christian Faith and Practice in the Modern World: Theology from an Evangelical Point of View*, ed. Mark A. Noll and David F. Wells. Grand Rapids: Eerdmans.

_____. 1992. *No Other Name: An Investigation into the Destiny of the Unevangelized.* Grand Rapids: Eerdmans.

_____. 1994. "Evangelical Responses to Salvation Outside the Church," *Christian Scholars Review* 24 (September 1994): 45-48.

_____. 1995a. "Inclusivism," in *What About Those Who Have Never Heard? Three Views on the Destiny of the Unevangelized*, ed. John Sanders. Downers Grove, IL: InterVarsity Press.

_____. 1995b. "Introduction," in *More Than One Way?* Ed. Dennis L. Okholm & Timothy R. Phillips. Grand Rapids: Zondervan, 1995.

_____. 2003. "A Free Will theist's Response to Talbott's Universalism." In in *Universal Salvation? The Current Debate,* ed Robin A. Parry and Christopher H. Partridge. Grand Rapids: William B. Eerdmans Publishing Co.

Schleiermacher, Friedrich.1928. *The Christian Faith,* ed. And trans. H. R. Mackintosh and J. S. Stewart. Edinburgh: T & T Clark.

Sanders, John, ed. 1995a. *What About Those Who Have Never Heard*? Downers Grove: InterVarsity Press.

Schnabel, Eckhard J. 2008. "Other Religions: *Saving or Secular*? In *Faith Comes by Hearing: A Response to Inclusivism.* Ed Morgan, Christopher W. and Peterson, Robert A.

Starkes, M. Thomas. 1978. *Today's World Religions.* New Orleans, La: Insight.

Only Jesus

_____. 1972. *Confronting Popular Cults.* Nashville: Broadman Press,

_____. 1981. *Islam and Eastern Religions: A Christian Response.* Nashville: Convention Press, 1981.

Smith, Ebbie C. 1984. *Balanced Church Growth: Church Growth Based on the Model of Servanthood.* Nashville: Broadman Press.

_____. 1998. "Contemporary Theology of Religions," in *Missiology: An Introduction to the Foundations, History, and Strategies of World Missions,* ed. John Mark Terry, Ebbie Smith, and Justice Anderson. Broadman & Holman.

_____. 2003, *Growing Healthy Churches: New Directions for Church Growth in the 21st Century* .Ft. Worth, TX: Church Starting Network.

Shedd, William G. T. 1886. *The Doctrine of Endless Punishment.* Minneapolis, MN: Klock & Klock Christian Publishers (Reprint 1980).

Shinn, Quillen Hamilton. Nd. "Affirmations of Universalism." http//www.auburn.edu/~allenkc/afmuniv.html.

Sproul, R. C. 1986, *Reason to Believe.* Grand Rapids: Zondervan.

Stetson, Eric. 2008. *Christian Universalism: God's Good News for al lPeople.* Sparkling Bay Books.

Stewart, Gary P. 2000. "Unmasking the Many Faces of Pluralism," in *The Fundamentals for the Twenty-First Century,* ed. Mal Couch. Grand Rapids: Kregel.

Strange, Daniel. 2002. *The Possibility of Salvation Among the Unevangelized: An Analysis of Inclusivism in Recent Evangelical Theology.* Cumbria, CA: Paternoster Publishing.

_____. 2003. "A Calvinist Response to Talbott's Universalism," in *Universal Salvation? The Current Debate,* ed Robin A. Parry and Christopher H. Partridge. Grand Rapids: William B. Eerdmans Publishing Co.

Swearer, Donald K. 1977. *Dialogue: The Key to Understanding Other Religions.* Philadelphia: The Westminster Press.

Talbott, Thomas. 1999. *The Inescapable Love of God.* Salem, OR: Universal Publishers/uPublish.

_____. 2003a. "Towards a Better Understanding of Universalism," in," *Universal Salvation: The Current Debate,* ed. Robin A. Parry and Christopher H. Partridge.

_____. 2003b. "Christ Victorius," in," *Universal Salvation: The Current Debate,* ed. Robin A. Parry and Christopher H. Partridge.

Sources

_____. 2003c. "A Pauline Interpretation of Divine Judgement," in," *Universal Salvation: The Current Debate,* ed. Robin A. Parry and Christopher H. Partridge.

_____. 2003d. "Reply to my Critics," in," *Universal Salvation: The Current Debate,* ed. Robin A. Parry and Christopher H. Partridge.

Tennent, Timothy C. 2002. *Christianity at the Religious Roundtable: Evangelicalism in Conversation with Hinduism, Buddhism, and Islam.* Grand Rapids: Baker, Academic.

_____. 2007. *Theology in the Context of World Christianity: How the Global Church is influencing the Way We thing About and Discuss Theology.* Grand Rapids: Zondervan.

Thayer, Thomas B. 1862. The *Theology of Universalism.* Boston: The Universalist Publication Press.

Tiénou, Tite. 1991. "Eternity in Their Hearts?" in *Through No Fault of Their Own,* ed. William V. Crockett and James G. Sigountos. Grand Rapids: Baker Book House.

_____. 2004. "Biblical Faith and Traditional Folk Religion," in In *Biblical Faith and Other Religions: An Evangelical Assessment,* ed. David W. Baker.

Tiessen, Terrance L. 2004. *Who Can Be Saved: Reassesing Salvation inChrist and World Religions.* Downers Grove, IL: InterVarsity Press.

Tippett, Alan R. 1967. *Solomon Island Christianity.* London: Lutterworth.

_____. 1969. *Verdict Theology in Missionary Theory.* Lincoln, Ill.: Lincoln Christian College Press.

_____. 1975. "The Meaning of Meaning," in *Christopaganism or Indigenous Christianity,* ed Tetasunao Yamamori and Charles R. Taber.

Toynbee, Arnold. 1957. *Christianity Among the Religions of the World.* New York: Charles Scribner's Sons.

Travis, Stephen H. 1980. *Christian Hope and the Future.* Downers Grove, IL: InterVarsity Press.

Trudeau, Richard. 2009. *Universalism 101: An Introduction for Leaders of Unitarian Universalist Congregations.* Published by Richard Trudeau.

Valea, Ernest. 2011. "Salvation and eternallife in world religions." http://www.compsrativereligion.com/salvation.html.

VanEngen, Charles. 1991. *God's Missionary People: Rethinking the Purpose of the Local Church.* Grand Rapids: Baker.

Only Jesus

_____. 1995. "The Uniqueness of Christ in Mission Theology," in *Christianity and the Religions: A Biblical Theology of World Religions*, eds. Edward Rommen and Harold Netland, Evangelical Missiological Society Series No. 2. William Carey Library.

Vatican II. *Gaudium et Spes.* http//www.vatican.va/archieve/hist_councils/ii_vatican-council/documents/vat-ii_cons_ 19651207_gaudium-et-spes_en.htm

Verkuyl, J. 1978. *Contemporary Missiology: An Introduction,* trans and ed Dale Cooper. Grand Rapids: Eerdmans Publishing Company.

Vincent, Ken R. 2005. *The Golden Thread: God's Promise of Universal Salvation.* New York: iUniverse.

Walsh, Michael. 2005. *Roman Catholicism: The Basics* (London and New York: Routledge.

Warfield, B. B. 1952. "Are They Few That Be Saved?" in *Biblical and Theological Studies* (Philadelphia: Presbyterian and Reformed Publishing Co.

Webster, William. "The Roman Catholic Teaching on Salvation and Justification,"

The WEF Manila Declaration. 1992. In *The Unique Christ in Our Pluralist World.* Ed Bruce J. Nicholls. Grand Rapids, MI: Baker Books, 1994.

Wells, David F. 1994. *God in the Wasteland: The Reality of Trut6h in a World of Fading Dreams.* Grand Rapids: Eerdmans.

Wenham, John. 1992. "The Case for Conditional Immortality," in *Universalism and the Doctrine of Hell: Papers Presented at the Fourth Edinburgh Conference on Christian Dogmatics.* Ed Nigel M. de S Cameron. Grand Rapids: Baker.

Wittmer, Michael E. 2011. *Christ Alone: An Evangelical Response to Rob Bell's Love Wins.* Grand Rapids: Edenridge press.

Wright, N. T. 1979. "Towards a Biblical View of Universalism," *Themelios* 4, 2 (January 1979): 54-57.

Wright, Chris. 1994. "The Unique Christ in the Plurality of Religions, in *The Unique Christ in Our Pluralist World.* Grand Rapids, MI: Baker Books.

Yadav, Bibhuti S. 1990. "Vashinavism on Hans Küng: A Hindu Theology of Religious Pluralism," in *Christianity Through Non-Christian Eyes*, ed. Paul J. Griffiths. Maryknoll, NY: Orbis Books.

Yamamamori, Tetasunao and Taber, Charles R. eds. 1975. *Christopaganism or Indigenous Christianity.* South Pasadena, CA: William Carey Library.

Sources

Yarbough, Robert W. 2004. "Jesus on Hell," in *Hell Under Fire*, ed Christopher W. Morgan and Robert A. Peterson. Grand Rapids: Zondervan.

Zegler, Albert. 1946. *The Christian Leader.* December 7, 1946.

http://www.comparativereligion.com/index.html ernest valea